Full Christianity

also by Richard W. Chilson, C.S.P.
published by Paulist Press

AN INTRODUCTION TO THE FAITH OF CATHOLICS
A LENTEN PILGRIMAGE—
DYING AND RISING IN THE LORD

Richard W. Chilson, C.S.P.

FULL CHRISTIANITY

A Catholic Response to Fundamental Questions

Paulist Press
New York/Mahwah

Copyright © 1985 by
The Missionary Society
of St. Paul the Apostle
in the State of New York

Library of Congress
Catalog Card Number: 84-62840

ISBN: 0-8091-2669-9

Published by Paulist Press
997 Macarthur Boulevard
Mahwah, New Jersey 07430

Printed and bound in the United States of America

Thanks to George and Barbara for their help

Contents

Preface
The Fundamentalist Challenge

We are witnessing today a resurgence of fundamentalist Christianity. Through the 1970's and the early 1980's fundamentalism, supposedly consigned to oblivion by the revolution of the 1960's, gained strength. The Moral Majority and the TV evangelists have equated fundamentalism with Christianity itself for many in our culture.

As a campus minister I have often been at the heart of this confrontation. Fundamentalist groups such as the Navigators, Campus Crusade for Christ, Intervarsity Christian Fellowship and others aggressively approach students including Catholics and other Christians in an attempt to win them over to the Gospel.

The message is put in such a way that a Christian from another persuasion often feels at a loss how to respond. The vocabulary, the techniques, the virtuosity in quoting Scripture. the important points are different. And they are unable to answer the challenge in such a way that their own faith is seen as valid.

But fundamentalists hardly hold an exclusive title. This book presents an alternative vision of Christianity—the catholic. In many ways the catholic position presents a clear alternative. For fundamentalism is basically a Protestant form of religion and exhibits classical Protestant themes.

Today many mainstream Protestant churches along with the Roman Catholic Church are re-examining the issues dividing us and are finding new answers. Both sides are moving away from the exaggerated positions of the past to discover a common ground in the middle. Thus although the book does not attempt a Protestant response to fundamentalism, mainstream Protestants may find themselves more in agreement with the catholic vision presented here than with the extreme form that fundamentalism presents.

Liberal Protestantism attempted to bridge the chasm between the faith and the modern world. How can modern people hear the good news of Jesus in a way they can understand and accept? Often the liberal position led to understanding the Gospel in new ways, but it also led to a watering down of Christianity and a departure from the traditional faith.

Reacting to the liberals, fundamentalists return to the basics. The would-be believer today faces a quandary. Do I abandon my position as a member of the twentieth century to embrace the traditional Christian faith, or do I accept a watered-down and rather feeble Christianity so that I may remain a citizen of this world? So fundamentalism puts the question.

But are the only alternatives a weak liberalized Christianity or an unthinking cleaving to the letter of Scripture? Catholicism provides another possibility. Catholics have clung to the fullness of the Christian faith. And Roman Catholicism today reaches out to the modern world in dialogue so that our faith may address the modern person.

Fundamentalists reject the catholic alternative, believing that catholicism polluted the faith through superstition and error. And indeed fundamentalists attack catholicism almost as much as liberalism. And they often seek Catholics as converts, seeing the conversion as an acceptance of true Christianity.

This book arises out of this campus situation but reaches far beyond the campus. Fundamentalists ask hard and difficult questions of catholics. Yet those questions can be answered.

And catholicism provides an alternative—one in which neither the traditional fundamentals are sacrificed nor the modern world is condemned. A catholic response to these questions shows how catholicism presents a different perspective on Christianity.

This book is "a" catholic response to fundamental questions. Overall it provides the official Roman Catholic faith but is not an official presentation of the faith. The way I choose to describe catholicism and critiques I may offer are not necessarily those of all catholics.

Indeed there could never be an official catholic response because such uniformity does not and should not exist in the faith. As Augustine once said, in essentials we agree, in other things diversity, but in all things charity. Other Catholics may disagree with my opinions: diversity gives the Church her catholicity. However the essentials presented here are the true catholic faith.[1]

---

1. This book distinguishes between catholicism and Roman Catholicism. Roman Catholicism is the most familiar representative of the catholic vision. But there are other catholics besides Roman Catholics; some Episcopalians, Lutherans and other Protestants see themselves as faithful to the catholic tradition. Catholic or catholicism with a small "c" states positions common to all catholics. Positions unique to the Roman Catholic Church are identified as Roman Catholic or use a capital "C".

Introduction
Two Visions: Catholic and Fundamentalist

Before considering individual questions let us examine some
basic characteristics of these two Christian visions. Certain ideas
will be repeatedly encountered in the specific questions. These
themes reveal the differences.

Two statements of Jesus ground these two Christian visions. At
one point Jesus says, "Whoever is not against you is with you."[1]
And at another time he says, "Whoever is not with you is
against you."[2] Catholicism at its best clings to the first statement
while fundamentalism takes the second to heart.

Whereas fundamentalism is exclusive (clinging only to what is
authentically and originally Christian), catholicism is inclusive
(seeking to include the whole world in the illumination of
Christ). Thus while catholicism is able to embrace the
fundamentals, fundamentalism is not able to embrace
catholicism. There is room for fundamentalism in catholicism,
and the Roman Catholic Church includes a number of
fundamentalist Catholics. But there is no place for a catholic
position in fundamentalism.

Fundamentalism arose because of concern that the established
Protestant churches were losing the faith in their attempts to
come to grips with the modern world. Liberalism was rampant
and fundamentalism called these churches back to the basics. It

---

1. Mk 9:40.
2. Mt 12:30.

derives its name from its insistence upon the ten fundamentals of Christianity drawn up by Madsen its founder.

The catholic attitude on the other hand seeks to illumine everything in the universe with the light of Christ. The Church, while preserving the purity of the Gospel, has not hesitated to allow the Gospel to come into contact with the culture, thus redeeming it.

Indeed Protestants criticize Catholicism for so easily assimilating things not originally Christian. We catholics view this as a kind of baptism. Thus St. Thomas Aquinas reworked the pagan thought of Aristotle making it a basis for Christian thought. Whereas fundamentalists see this as a betrayal of the Gospel, catholics believe that it allows the Gospel to transform the world.

Basically the fundamentalist is pessimistic toward the world while the catholic is optimistic. As G.K. Chesterton once noted, two people observe a half glass of water: the optimist sees it half full, the pessimist half empty. So the catholic looks at the world and sees it as the glorious creation of God. Yes, it is fallen, but, full of kinks though it is, it still proclaims the handiwork of its maker.

The fundamentalist sees the world perverted by sin. All is warped. Humanity can accomplish no good on its own. And what seems good is even more suspect since it is likely the devil's work. A catholic can see all the good in humanity and give thanks to God for it. Of course humanity apart from Christ is sinful and will sin. But it still accomplishes much that is beautiful: God does not create trash. Such attitudes can lead to a certain amount of gullibility, whereas the fundamentalist falls into a paranoid belief in the power of the devil.

Classically the argument between catholics and fundamentalists concerns grace. For the catholic grace perfects nature just as

Jesus perfects (brings to fulfillment) Israel.[3] Humanity is basically good, and that goodness finds fulfillment in Christianity.

Fundamentalism on the other hand, believing in the total depravity of creation, insists that grace replaces our sinful nature. There is no continuum from humanity to Christ. We must be totally re-created. There is no goodness to build upon. This leads to a rather dim view of everything not specifically Christian. This is not to deny that there are optimists among fundamentalists and pessimists among catholics. But the dominant theologies are by and large as stated here.

Further implications of this split can be found in the major dogmatic emphases. Catholicism emphasizes the incarnation— that God became a human being. He came to dwell with us. He likes us. He enjoys us. Catholics see great implications in this doctrine. As Jesus became a man at a certain time, so he is with us today. He is present in his Church. And he is involved with making the entire universe full of himself so that he becomes all in all.

For fundamentalists the crux of the matter is the doctrine of the atonement—Jesus' death for our sins. Of course it is not a matter of either group denying either doctrine: rather it is the emphasis laid upon one or the other. For the fundamentalist creation is so warped that only the atoning death of Jesus can put it right. The cross becomes the great event in history— there God accepts Jesus' death as payment for sin.

Now catholics believe in the atonement, but we prefer a different interpretation of it. We go back to the roots of the word: "at-one-ment." On the cross Jesus brings God and humanity together; he reconciles us to God. And catholics have

---

3. Mt 5:17–19.

great reverence for the cross; it is one of our major religious symbols. But we see the cross in the light of the incarnation—as he has taken upon our life, so now he takes on our death, transforming it to fulfill our fondest dreams.

In these doctrines again we can see the different visions. Incarnation is taking on the world. Atonement is a contradiction—a denying of the world; the cross is the great stumbling block, as Paul says.[4] Neither group rejects either dogma, but each chooses to view Christianity primarily through the lenses of one or the other.

We see a difference of emphasis upon what is important in both groups as well. While at least traditionally catholicism has emphasized sacraments, fundamentalism emphasizes the word and preaching. Again neither denies the validity of either word or sacrament: it is a matter of emphasis. I had to say traditionally because today Catholicism lays renewed emphasis upon the word. But we are still by and large a sacramental Church. And fundamentalism does not really accept the traditional Christian understanding of sacrament.[5]

These key differences will crop up again and again in the specific questions. It is the difference between an insistence upon roots or fullness. For the fundamentalist the only important thing is the Gospel in its purity. For the catholic it is necessary to allow the Gospel to be heard by the world so that the world may be transformed. We are thus concerned with the fullness of the Gospel.

These are radically different visions calling for a choice. How do you prefer to view the world? Is it totally depraved apart from Christ? What are you going to say then about non-Christian culture, art, philosophy, music, let alone religion?

---

4. 1 Cor 1:18.
5. See question 4A.

But if you find beauty in the world, if you recognize the Creator in a glorious sunset, if you hear his voice in the world's music and art, then you are closer to the catholic persuasion. As you explore the following questions ask yourself how you feel and which vision most captures the love of God revealed to us in Christ Jesus.[6]

6. Jn 3:16.

Scripture, Authority and Revelation

1A. Where can we find the good news of Christianity today?

Good news is the essence of Christianity. Jesus announced he had come to proclaim the good news of the Kingdom of God. His preaching was filled with this good news; his miracles and signs were experiences of the good news. People followed Jesus, attracted by the good news.

For his disciples, Jesus himself—in his death and resurrection—epitomizes the good news. And they carried this good news into the world of their day. So authentic Christianity must always be characterized by this element of good news.

If what you hear as Christianity does not sound like good news but rather is bad news, then it can hardly be authentic. It is a perversion of the original Gospel—an Old English word which means "good news." This is not to deny difficult aspects to the good news, but in spite of everything it must sound more like good news than bad news to be authentically Gospel.

This good news has become essentially the person and life of Jesus Christ. The good news is not simply a message but an encounter with a human being. And the best way to encounter a human being is through a human being or a community. So the best way to come into contact with the good news is through a Christian community. There the good news has been passed on and lives today. Through these Christians as through the original disciples we come to know and experience Jesus Christ.

How is this good news communicated in the Church? It is first of all communicated through a proclamation—the story of Jesus, who he is, what he says and what he accomplishes. But it is communicated as well through the community—the sense of love and care for one another, the community's mission to the world of service and love. It is communicated through the individual Christians. Each has a unique story of his or her encounter with Jesus Christ. It is communicated through the prayer and the worship of the community—Jesus nourishing and transforming his people.

In the earliest Christian Church this good news was at times communicated through the written word. Paul, the great missionary, sent letters to his different churches to explain the faith and correct misunderstandings. Other apostles as well wrote letters to the Christian churches.

As time went by the communities which cherished and passed down the disciples' recollections of Jesus and the stories of Jesus himself began to set them down in written form. Eventually these documents circulated through the different Christian communities and were treasured. Finally gathered together and declared Scripture by the Church, today Scripture is a primary vehicle for the good news.

Indeed today the good news in its most authoritative form is the Bible. For us the Bible is the very word of God. On this point all Christians agree. Then to find the good news would it not simply do to read the Bible?

While the Bible proclaims the good news in the normative way, the reading of the Bible is not the whole of the good news. The real good news is the encounter with Jesus Christ—a person. The experiencing of the good news is richer than a mere hearing of the word of God. And the fullness of human experience can only be communicated by other human beings;

thus only in a Christian community can the fullness of the good news be received.

Besides, why should we accept the Bible as a normative expression of the good news? By what authority is it so? It does not say so itself. Nowhere in the Bible is there a passage that says this list of writings is the authentic word of God. And even if it did, why should we believe it? Living as we do in a society permeated by Christian attitudes we tend to accept the Bible as the word of God unthinkingly. But who authenticates it?

The Bible is the product of the Christian Church. It was written by her members, and she at a certain point decided which books belonged in it and decreed it normative. The community preceded the Scriptures, gave them birth, preserved them and finally declared them Scripture. The Bible belongs to the Church as one of her most precious gifts from God. She declared it normative and allows it to judge her thought and behavior—but she possesses it, not it her.

And how are we to interpret or understand the Bible? Is it self-explanatory or self-evident? The Bible is hardly a systematic, well thought out presentation of the faith. It is a series of books written by different people at different times, embodying various philosophies and viewpoints.

Two thousand years of Christian controversy should be enough to bury the idea that the Bible is self-evident to anyone with an open mind. From the beginning Christians, even with the aid of the Bible, have had great difficulty articulating just what God is saying.

Does it not make sense that the community which gave birth to and proclaimed these writings as Scripture should also be the proper interpreter? The community introduces us to the Scriptures as her cherished treasure—the inspired Word of God. She helps us read and understand these Scriptures by sharing her wisdom gained through centuries of meditation, prayer, reflection, discussion and argument.

Indeed we only come to understand Scripture through the mediation of a Christian community whether it be Catholic, Protestant or fundamentalist. For one would not necessarily arrive at the fundamentalist any more than the Catholic position simply by reading the Scriptures from one's own supposedly neutral experience.

1B. Which is the authentic Christian community?

A great many Christian communities compete and sometimes manifest open antagonism toward each other. Which of these many churches is authentic? Obviously part of your choice must be made from experience. You need to find a community that indeed can nourish and challenge you. But experience cannot be all we take into account. For how can we be sure that an experience with a Christian community no matter how wonderful it might be is authentic Christian experience? We need guidelines with which to evaluate the different communities.

Some Christians might answer this question by saying that first you read the Scriptures and then choose a community closest to those Scriptures. This is a possible way to proceed, yet the community in some way precedes and gives birth to Scripture.[1] While Scripture might validate the community, it is the community that must interpret the Scripture.

Traditionally Christians have spoken of four marks of the true Church. We find these marks in the Nicene Creed, professed by all the mainstream churches of Christendom and held as the

---

1. See question 1A.

official articulation of the Christian faith. A group rejecting this Creed should immediately be suspect since they are going against an overwhelming consensus. The Creed professes that the true Church of Christ is one, holy, catholic and apostolic. Let us consider each of these marks in turn.

First, the true Christian Church is united. Jesus creates unity among people. And his community must be united as well. Of course one of the major scandals of Christendom is the divisions between the different Churches—a history of heresy, schism and discord. Most Christians although disagreeing over various things at least hold this Nicene Creed in common.

But what sign of unity do we then have? True unity should go beyond some invisible amorphous group who share a Creed. How is such a unity perceived by those outside the faith? We speak of marks of the Church—something that can be seen or experienced. We find a plethora of Christian communities who cannot even worship together. And who draws up the criteria for membership in this invisible united Church? Do we not end up with a series of Churches allied on the basis of who thinks alike? Is Christianity a matter of accepting as the truth the first version heard from the first Christian stumbled upon? Or, even worse, is Christianity ultimately accepting and believing what you choose?

The unity of the Church, as most Christians agree, needs to be manifest concretely. And one ultimate sign of Christian unity is sharing in the Eucharist. Such unity the different Christian Churches seek today. Our insight and understanding of the Gospel deepens as we share with one another, praying that the day of full Christian unity may one day dawn.

A concrete sign of Christian unity dates back to Jesus who appointed Peter as the leader of the apostles.[2] Peter in the

---

2. Mt 16:16–19.

course of his mission ended up in Rome. And traditionally Christians have seen the bishop of Rome as his successor. This bishop who is called the Pope is considered throughout Christian history as a visible sign of unity: those Christians who are united to the Pope are in unity with one another.

Even churches such as the Orthodox and Protestant that are today divided from the Pope and his community recognize him as a symbol of Christian unity. Indeed the quarrel is not so much over the office itself as how that office has developed in the Roman Church. In any attempt at reunion the papacy will have to be re-examined and redefined. But for today the only community possessing this sign of Christian unity is the Roman Catholic Church, and for that reason alone this Church is worthy of investigation.

The second mark of the Christian Church is holiness. Jesus told his disciples that they might recognize a true follower by means of their fruits.[3] What are the signs of holiness in the various Christian communities?

The Roman Catholic tradition manifests countless examples of holiness and sanctity in the panoply of saints. Consider the great mystics such as Teresa of Avila or John of the Cross. Or witness reformers such as Francis of Assisi who altered the course not only of the Church but the Western world. Closer to our own time Pope John XXIII initiated reforms still occurring within the Catholic community, and he inspired similar reforms in other Christian communities, spurring Christian hopes for reunion. There are family people such as Thomas More; worldly saints like Philip Neri; American saints such as Frances Cabrini. We might even point out neurotic saints who give hope to us fellow neurotics. And today in our world there are outstanding examples of holiness such as Mother Teresa of Calcutta.

---

3. Mt 7:16.

Apostolicity is the third mark of the Church. Where does this community come from? What are its roots, its history, its tradition? And is the community in continuity with the original faith of the apostles?

The Roman Catholic and Orthodox Churches literally have a continuous lineage back to the original apostles. Known as the apostolic succession, it refers to the unbroken linkage of the imposition of hands in ordination—any bishop today was ordained by a bishop who in turn was ordained by another all the way back to the original apostles. In this limited sense apostolicity refers also to a continuity of faith throughout the ages. It guarantees the faith of a community today is the same as that original faith of the apostles.

Finally the authentic Christian community is marked by catholicity. Catholic means universal. It is not the sole possession of the Roman Church—all churches that profess the Creed call themselves catholic in this broader sense. Catholicity is a mark of how open a particular Christian church is to all cultures and peoples. Is there room for the whole of human experience within a particular church? And is there communion between different peoples with their unique experiences within the Church?

The Roman Catholic Church at her best illustrates wonderfully the principle of catholicity. Look at the daring way in which Christianity was transplanted from its Hebrew roots into the Greco-Roman world. While Jesus originally viewed himself as the fulfillment of the Israelite experience, the early Church saw that he fulfilled as well the hopes and dreams of Greece and Rome. Unfortunately with the Reformation the Roman Church became defensive and restrictive. In the great missionary expeditions to Asia she forced a Western form of Christianity on the peoples, and perhaps for this reason Christianity has not been greatly accepted in Asia.

Today through the Second Vatican Council the Roman Church is reclaiming her catholic principle and making strides to separate Western chauvinism from the Gospel. She recognizes the unique heritages and traditions of her various peoples, and already African and Asian Christians are bringing new life and vitality to a moribund European Church.

A Christian community should both acknowledge your own traditions, customs and experiences, and open you in turn to a wealth of experience from other peoples and times. While the mark of apostolicity guarantees that the original faith has been preserved, the mark of catholicity means that all things are being drawn to and illumined by Christ.

1C. Does the Pope replace Scripture as the final authority for Catholics?

In the past Catholics might have feared that they would have to answer this question in the affirmative. For during the last few centuries the papacy underwent a tremendous development which exalted the Pope as an imperial ruler. The doctrine of papal infallibility[4] and the power concentrated in the Pope's hands gave the impression of an autocratic ruler accountable to no one but God.

In addition Catholics possessed a general ignorance of Scripture which even today is not eradicated. But the truth is that the idea of the centrality of Scripture to Christian life is a rather recent and Protestant development. It is dependent upon the availability of the printed word (which did not occur until the Reformation) and a general literacy (also a modern phenomenon).

Catholicism had developed other devotions not dependent upon the written word. And in reaction to the Reformation the

---

4. See question 1G.

reading of Scripture as a practice of Catholic piety was not stressed. Today the Second Vatican Council stresses Scripture's role in nourishing Christian life. Certainly Catholics can no longer be accused of relegating Scripture to second place in their faith, nor can Catholics be acquitted for being ignorant of the Scriptures.

However this question focuses upon the papacy and its authority within the Catholic tradition. The question is really over the final earthly authority for a Christian—should it be a Pope (or some Church leader), the Church itself, or Scripture?

Consider the relationship between Scripture and the Church as stated in the Constitution on Divine Revelation of the Second Vatican Council. First, the revelation of God in its fullness is Jesus Christ himself. He reveals the will of God and God's love for us. He entrusts this revelation to his apostles who in turn hand it on to their successors as the divine tradition. This handing on takes place already in the New Testament.[5] The New Testament Scriptures are a crystallization of this tradition which precedes them. And the Scriptures must be understood in the light of the living tradition which both produced them and interprets them.

> Sacred tradition and Sacred Scripture form one sacred deposit of the word of God, committed to the Church. Holding fast to this deposit the entire holy people, united with their shepherds, remain always steadfast in the teaching of the Apostles, in the common life, in the breaking of the bread and in prayers, so that holding to, practicing and professing the heritage of the faith, it becomes on the part of the bishops and the faithful a remarkable common effort.[6]

---

5. 1 Cor 11:23; 2 Thes 2:15.
6. De Revelatione 2:10.

Here the Church stresses tradition and Scripture not as two sources of revelation but rather as two streams flowing from the one revelation who is Jesus. We see the holistic nature of Catholicism. Christianity is not simply a matter of hearing and obeying the word of God. It includes as well the common life, the breaking of the bread, and the prayers. Within this community life the Scriptures are appreciated and understood.

Now Scripture because it is inspired[7] has become a norm for the Church along with tradition. Thus Scripture judges the Church in her actions and teachings. The Scriptures are normative, and therefore the Church or the Pope may not teach anything in conflict with them. So Catholicism does not put the Pope or the Church above the Scriptures.

1D. How is Scripture to be read and interpreted?

Who is to interpret the Scriptures? Within the Catholic community the task of interpreting and discerning the word of God is entrusted to the teaching office of the Church which includes the Pope and the bishops. While this may seem snobbish in this democratic age, consider what is involved.

The Scriptures were written over a thousand year period in a culture two thousand years removed from our own. During the course of their existence they have been translated into various other languages and consulted to illumine countless situations. Besides by their nature they are not a systematic presentation of the faith. Various books provide differing viewpoints. For example, it is not easy to reconcile the theology of Paul with Matthew or with Hebrews.

Can their authentic interpretation be left simply to people who believe that because they can read they can understand the

---

7. See question 1F.

problems involved? One might as well say that the average high school sophomore's interpretation of Hamlet is as authentic as that of the actor who has wrestled with the play in numerous productions or the scholar who has given his or her life to the study of Shakespeare. An authentic interpretation of revelation needs a teaching authority in continuity ultimately with the apostles and with Jesus himself.

This does not mean that Catholics should not read the Scriptures and attempt to reach their own understanding. Indeed the Catholic church allows a wide interpretation of the Scriptures. Of all the doctrinal statements of the Catholic church throughout history only a handful have focused upon the interpretation of a specific passage of Scripture. And doctrines[8] simply set up the boundaries within which we may understand Scripture—they tell us when we have gone too far, when the text can not support our conclusion. Within those boundaries we are free to forge our own interpretation. And the variety of scriptural commentary within the Church today attests to the amount of freedom available.

But how are we to read Scripture overall? With what understanding and framework do we approach it? This is the work of the magisterium, the Church's teaching office. Any Christian group including fundamentalists provides such a framework. The question is: Whose credentials are to be trusted? The bishops have given their lives to the meditation and study of the word of God and of the Catholic tradition. They are advised by theologians and scholars expert in their fields. They take into consideration the views of the Catholic people as a whole both today and throughout history. They are hardly arbitrary in their teachings. And they are promised the guidance of the Holy Spirit.[9]

---

8. See question 1E.
9. Jn 20:22–23.

There has been a tremendous revival of interest and study of Scripture within modern Catholicism. In 1943 Pope Pius XII opened the doors for Catholic Scripture scholars to bring all the resources of twentieth century textual criticism and archeology to bear on their study of Scripture. As a result within a few years Catholic Scripture scholarship has grown by leaps and bounds.

Ecumenically Catholicism and the Protestant Churches are moving closer together in our understanding of Scripture and therefore of the faith we share. We are also rediscovering our roots in the common experience of Israel and so are moving toward a renewed appreciation and understanding of Judaism, our mother faith. On the grass roots level there has been a great upsurge of interest in Scripture. And of course we encounter the Scriptures at the very center of our Christian life in the Eucharist. There through the course of three years the Christian community prays and meditates upon the breadth of Scriptures and is fed by the word of God just as by the Eucharist itself.

1E. Haven't Catholics added doctrines to revelation not in Scripture?

Over the centuries as a result of historical circumstances doctrines have become an important part of Christianity, and nowhere more so than Roman Catholicism. Some might assume that in Catholicism dogma has usurped the place of Scripture. But dogma serves an important though limited function.

Dogma is a Greek word meaning "a statement." So it is a definition of the faith. Historically dogmas haven't defined the faith so much as set up boundaries that stake out its limits. For example, Christians believe that Jesus is both fully human and fully divine: he is both God and man. Now while that may seem like a definition it really only sets boundaries to our understanding of Jesus. We can not conceive of Jesus in such a way that we deny either his divinity or his humanity. But within those limits there is plenty left to wonder about, and even today theologians are developing modern understandings of Jesus faithful to these original dogmas.

Consider how dogma arose in early Christianity. Christian revelation in its fullness is Jesus Christ himself. The disciples experienced Jesus and his resurrection and they then began to spread what they had received to others. They spoke of Jesus, his teachings, and his works, and they told of his death and resurrection. This preaching then became part of an oral tradition carefully passed on to and cherished by each new Christian community. Eventually a written tradition appeared as well, and later these writings were gathered together and declared by the Church to be her Scriptures—she claimed them to be inspired.[10]

Now at this time as well the early Christian Church was moving from being a development out of Israel and her experience and was taking upon herself the Greco-Roman culture and thought of the early converts. The Christians were not successful in winning Jews, but largely through Paul's mission great numbers of non-Jews entered the early Church. These conversions brought the Church out of the Jewish world into the cosmopolitan Roman Empire where Greek philosophy was dominant. To address this world and win it over the Church began translating ideas that had come to flower in Hebrew culture into the alien world of Greco-Roman culture. As in any attempt at change some resisted the whole idea, but thankfully the Church at large adopted this translation process and Christianity grew.

The Scriptures, both those of Israel and the new Christian writings, by and large reflected the Hebrew context out of which they arose. The Bible is hardly a logical presentation of

---

10. See question 1F.

either Israel's or the Christian faith. Questions arose concerning Jesus and his message. This is no fault of the Scriptures. Systematic thought is a Greek obsession, while Hebrew thought developed along other lines. But now if people trained in Greek ways of thinking attempt to understand the Scriptures they need help translating from one way of thought to the other. Dogma is the result.

Further, as Christians presented their faith to the Greco-Roman world new questions arose demanding answers if the faith were to be properly understood. Who was Jesus? Was Jesus a God who had come among us? Was he an ordinary man divinized at some point in his life? Was he simply an inspired teacher? And if Jesus is God as the Christians said, and if God was also Father and Holy Spirit, are there three gods or only one? Many such questions arose, and the debate grew exciting and even dangerous, since people were not above killing for the truth as they saw it.

These debates made it necessary from time to time for the Church to convene in council to clarify the issues. In these councils the earliest (and most of the important) Christian doctrines were hammered out. This entire process is a necessary translation of revelation using the language of Greek (neo-Platonic) philosophy. Far from ending discussion, the dogmas merely set up boundaries for a discussion that continued within them. The dogma defined acceptable orthodox belief. To deny the dogmatic definition was to find oneself a heretic and outside the faith. However, within the Church, the debates and the councils they engendered thrived throughout the first six hundred years of Christianity.

Dogma forms part of every Christian community from the Roman Catholic to the fundamentalist. Fundamentalist belief that Scripture is inspired is just as nonscriptural a dogma as any other.

The doctrine of the Trinity as commonly defined is not found in the Bible. For we assert that there are three persons in one God—a statement not found in Scripture. It does not contradict Scripture. And our understanding of the doctrine arose from what is revealed in Scripture. But it is a result of the Greek rethinking of Christianity. Looking back we can read Scripture and see evidence for the doctrine of the Trinity, but the doctrine itself is not there, developing only in the third century.

Now most Christians accept the Trinity as a fundamental doctrine; some believe it is the central doctrine. Yet it is not found in Scripture. So if a Christian accepts the doctrine of the Trinity he or she must implicitly believe that the Church's wrestling with this problem and her solution to it is legitimate. Few believe that the Trinity is a corruption of the pure faith of the Scriptures. Instead they might say that the Church had the right if not the obligation to proclaim this doctrine to protect the true faith. But when does this obligation cease? Did God protect the Church only until the third century? Or is that protection, that assurance that we have not received a perverted version of Christianity, still with the Christian Church today?

Common sense would say that if God took the trouble (and death on a cross can only be called trouble) to reveal himself in Jesus, and Jesus in turn entrusted this revelation to his followers, then there must be some assurance that the revelation will be protected from betrayal or loss. Catholics believe that God does indeed protect his revelation in such a way. How can we find the true revelation of Jesus? It is preserved through the ages by the community bearing his name.

Nothing has been added to the original revelation. Dogmas are simply articulations of that revelation. Most of these major dogmas are set forth in the traditional Creeds of Christianity, especially the Nicene Creed.

1F. What does it mean to say that Scripture is inspired?

Even a casual acquaintance with Christianity reveals that
Christians do not think of the Bible as an ordinary book. The
Bible is the word of God, and we speak of the Scriptures as
inspired by God.

The word of God is central to the Judeo-Christian tradition.
The law which established and governed Israel was considered
directly communicated by God to Moses and through him to
the people. The law, or torah, is the most sacred revelation of
God to Israel, embodying God's vision of what Israel is to be.

Later the prophets claimed to speak the word of God to the
people in order to comfort, challenge or draw them back to the
law. Throughout Israel's history God reveals himself first of all
through the events of history, but in addition to this direct
revelation, an accompanying word draws meaning from the
events. Although Israel valued the word of God, she above all
discerned the revelation in the events of her history.

For Christians the full expression of God's word is Jesus
himself. This idea is fully set forth in John's Gospel which
beings with a prologue—a Christian retelling of the creation
story with the Word center-stage and the further revelation that
this Word through whom the entire universe was created is no
other than Jesus. He is the Word made human flesh.

God's word is not simply a word in our ordinary understanding
of the term. Words are fairly lifeless entities in our culture. The
word John speaks of is closer to the powerful transforming
word of poetry than to the prosaic notion of word common
today. And of crucial importance: this Word has taken flesh—
he lives and acts among us. The word enfleshed in Jesus is an
active, dynamic, transforming Word. It is much more than the
word of a book, even if that book is the Bible, or the spoken
word no matter how persuasive. This Word creates the universe
and sustains it in being.

While the Word of God refers to God's revelation in Israel's history or his full disclosure in the person of Jesus, we must also take into account the various words by which we encounter this Word of God. Jesus uses words to speak of the Kingdom of God and to point the way to that Kingdom.

These words were passed down through the Christian community until they assumed final form in the written Gospels. And in the passage the words were sometimes changed, for Christians do not think of the Word of God in the sense of a dead word but rather a living Word.

There is a distinction between the Word of God and the words used by the Scriptural authors to communicate the Word; blurring this distinction distorts the traditional Christian understanding of inspiration. If we say that the words of Scripture are themselves the word of God we shall have to treat Scripture itself as the revelation of God. But for Christians the Bible is not the revelation of God—Jesus Christ is. The Bible passes on that revelation.

Yet some treat the Bible as though it is the be-all and the end-all of Christianity. When they do this they are more like Muslims than Christians. For Islam the Koran or sacred book is the direct word of God and treated accordingly. Compare the fundamentalists of Islam such as the Khomeini in Iran with Christian fundamentalists—they have much in common. But such idolatry of Scripture is contrary to most of Christendom. The Bible is our holy book, but Jesus is the revelation of God to us: he is the center of our faith.

God is the author of Scripture in the sense that God is the origin of Scripture: God gives rise to the Scriptures. The Scriptures communicate the revelation of God. They do so not directly, but rather through a human author who is God's instrument. The actual words, concepts and world view of a piece of Scripture are those of the document's author or authors. Through those words God reveals himself.

But if God is the author of Scripture, does this mean then that Scripture has no errors in it? Fundamentalists make this claim; witness the controversy over evolution which seems to contradict the seven-day creation.[11] They claim that the Bible is literally true. Now when you make such a claim you are going to have to deal with a great many more problems than evolution.

For the Scriptures are the products of diverse people from diverse times with diverse points of view. Indeed one can argue that not all the books of Scripture agree with one another: Paul is set against Matthew, James against Paul. Besides this there seem to be contradictions within certain books of the Bible, and what we know from outside sources such as archeology sometimes conflicts with the biblical events. Nor have we yet taken into consideration biblical notions of psychology, science, history or other disciplines which do not correlate with current knowledge.

Some Protestants have abandoned belief in scriptural inspiration. Against these liberals fundamentalists wage war. Catholics were not so quick to abandon the traditional ideas of inspiration and inerrancy in regard to Scripture, and the Catholic position today steers a middle course between the fundamentalists' rigidity and the liberals' surrender. Catholicism holds on to the inspiration of Scripture on the one hand while accepting the human authors of Scripture as products of their time and culture, subject to human limitations.[12]

God uses the limited human being to communicate the good news. Human limitations do not prove an obstacle; just as in Jesus he was able to assume a human body with all the limitations of our humanity and yet communicate himself to us,

---

11. Gn 1:1–31.
12. For example, Matthew (Mt 27:9–10) attributes a quotation to Jeremiah that actually comes from Zechariah (Zech 11:12–13).

so he communicates his word through human authors. God works through our ideas, philosophies, and cultural limitations to reveal himself.

To understand what is revealed we must discover what the original author intended. For example, did the author of Jonah—where a man is swallowed by a whale—intend to tell of a mircle concerning a real man who was regurgitated, or did he use a fable known throughout Near Eastern cultures to show that God's love is not limited to Israel but includes all his creatures—a truth that Israel as well as Christianity has had a hard time swallowing?

If the genre is history we should read it as history. But what is the writer's understanding of history? The discipline has changed greatly and we cannot expect the author to have an understanding that did not develop until two thousand years later. History to Luke is quite different from a modern historian's conception. To judge Luke by modern historical standards results in confusion and difficulty. To understand Luke according to his own conception of his task allows us to discern the revelation of the word through the words.

Catholics believe that the Bible is free from error in what it tells us concerning God. When it speaks of other matters it uses the concepts and ideas of the human author and should be judged accordingly. Scripture does not teach biology, psychology, or science. It communicates God to us. To use it for other ends misuses it. The Catholic position maintains the traditional Christian faith that God is the author of Scripture yet allows us to live in the twentieth century.

The Bible is the living word of God. Christians do not regard it primarily as a record of past events. To read the Bible as a Christian is to encounter the word of God spoken to you today. When we read what Jesus said to the scribes and Pharisees we do so not to find out about some long past debate, but to discover what Jesus might have to say to us today, for the temptations and failings of the scribes and Pharisees are universal temptations.

Scripture comes alive for us. Suddenly out of these distant times the word leaps over the centuries, speaking compellingly to our present situation. Again not the concrete words of Scripture are the word—the Word is Christ who encounters us in the hearing of these words. God is not the author only at the time of its original writing. God is the author today as his living word meets us through the mediation of these written words.

This idea of the living word of God makes the Bible unique for Christians. Other books may inspire us. And there will be times when the Bible may not. But no other book is inspired for us; no other book is the word of God; no other book is alive in this way. In Catholic worship everyone stands when the Gospel is proclaimed. We stand not simply out of reverence, but as a sign of the resurrection; we acknowledge that we are in the presence of the risen Christ, who speaks to us today with the same presence and power with which he originally spoke the words preserved in the Gospels.

1G. What does it mean to say that the Pope is infallible?

This question compliments its predecessor. If the term inspiration has been used by Christians to apply to Scripture, Catholics have applied the term infallible to the Church and to the Pope in particular. To many the two terms seem much the same. Can we say that Scripture is infallible? Or on the other hand that the Pope is inspired? Actually we can not interchange the two terms for they mean quite different things.

Infallibility is a guarantee that the Christian community will not lose or pervert the revelation given it by Jesus Christ. Jesus appoints his disciple Peter as the leader of the community and then promises Peter that the gates of hell will never prevail against the Church.[13]

But lest Christians become over-confident of this protection, bear in mind what happened to Peter right after he received Jesus' promise. Jesus speaks about his approaching death and Peter tries to dissuade him from going to Jerusalem. Jesus turns to Peter and says, "Get behind me, Satan! You think like man and not like God."[14] This protection against the jaws of hell is no guarantee that the Church or Peter will always do the right thing.

Saying that the Church is infallible means that in its official teaching and life she can not betray or lose the vision entrusted to her. When Christians throughout the ages have had to come together to decide an issue of faith, the Holy Spirit has guided them in preserving the true faith. There have been many necessary decisions in the course of Christian history. It was easy to make a mistake, not so easy to arrive at the truth.

During this time the bishop of Rome, claiming succession from Peter himself (who died in Rome), emerged as the sign of unity among Christians. And the power of the papacy began to develop. In the Middle Ages the Eastern and Western Churches split apart, partly as a result of the increasing power of the Pope and his disregard for the apostolic traditions of the East. In the Western Church the role of the Pope assumed greater importance. Although the great schism was seen as a catastrophe, yet the Church, rallying around the Pope, saw itself still as the true Church.

The East was more cautious and conservative, feeling, since the body of the Church was now split, that a truly ecumenical council (a gathering of all the bishops, the Church's official

---

13. Mt 16:16–19.
14. Mt 16:23.

teachers) was impossible. No longer could dogmas be decreed through a council. Thus Eastern Christianity is frozen at the last ecumenical council and no further dogmatic definitions have occurred.

In the West since the Church held the symbol of unity in the Pope there have been further councils—about one every century. And throughout the Middle Ages the office of the papacy continued to develop, unfortunately taking as its model the institution of king in the secular society.

In the modern world the power of the Pope was gradually restricted to the spiritual realm. In the nineteenth century the Pope lost the last of the Vatican States and could no longer be considered a temporal ruler at all. But within the Church more and more power was concentrated in his hands.

Finally the First Vatican Council declared that the Pope is infallible. In other words the infallibility which had always been a part of the Church was now defined to be in a special way found in the Pope himself. This would seem to have been the end of the development.

But what is papal infallibility? When the Pope teaches with all his authority as the leader of the Church, he is prevented from proclaiming an error in faith and morals. When the Pope teaches in any less authoritative way—as is usually the case—he is not infallible. Thus far only two papal statements qualify as ex cathedra (meaning from the papal throne)—the Immaculate Conception and the Assumption of Mary.[15] The doctrine explicitly extends to the Pope what had already been believed of the Pope and bishops in council—and conciliar statements are other examples of infallible doctrines in the Catholic Church.

---

15. See question 5E.

Infallibility is not the same as inspiration. God is not the author of these statements as he is of Scripture. Infallibility only guarantees that in such statements the Pope or the Church acting in council (the situation of most defined dogmas) is preserved from teaching error.

Many Catholics believe that the days of the Pope's speaking infallibly are already behind us. Most Christian dogmas arose out of crises in attempting to define the faith and so were the products of the Church's early centuries. The definition of papal infallibility could be seen as an attempt to build up the papacy's spiritual power at the very time it was losing its worldly power. And even this image of the papacy has now been consigned to history.

John XXIII, elected as an interim Pope, is responsible for moving the Church from the imperial model to a new image of the papacy. First, he shocked the Church by calling for a council. Many people felt that the days of the councils were over, and they wondered why a council was necessary. There was no great crisis facing the Church, and even if there were, could not the Pope handle it himself? But John wanted a different kind of council—a pastoral council rather than a dogmatic council. The council would consider how the Church might best serve and proclaim the Gospel to this day and age.

In the council itself the issue of papal infallibility came up again, and the bishops realized that the First Vatican Council had left its work unfinished. The definition of papal infallibility must be seen in perspective. The original definition was too one-sided.

The Second Vatican Council complemented the doctrine by re-emphasizing the Pope as the head of the Church in collegiality with the bishops. The Pope does not stand alone. He is the sign of unity, but he is joined together with the entire Church and is aided in his teaching office by the college of bishops and by the

Church as a whole. Thus the definition of episcopal collegiality helped create a new model for the papacy.

But Pope John himself forged the new image. He downplayed the image of ruler and legislator and he made the papacy a sign of Christ's love and compassion in the world. He and his successors for the first time in centuries left the confines of the Vatican to meet the people. In his encyclicals he spoke out on the issues of peace and justice. John reclaimed the images of shepherd and pastor.

John's successors have followed in his image and enriched it: pastoral men concerned with the spiritual and temporal welfare of all the world's peoples in addition to being the leader of the Roman Catholic Church. Today the Pope speaks not to define and condemn, but more often to cry out against the injustices of the world, to call all people to compassion, forgiveness and love, to be a sign of peace and reconciliation, a sign of Christ in the world.

This change of image does not mean that infallibility is lost or that it is unnecessary. We are now almost two thousand years from the revelation of Jesus Christ. We have a Scripture. But the Scripture is not always clear, nor easy to understand. Without the guarantee of infallibility there would be no hope of finding the authentic message of Jesus.

And without the Pope—the sign of Christian unity—we could not be assured of being in continuity with the revelation of Jesus. The image and the office of the Pope have changed throughout history and they are changing today. But as Protestants and Catholics alike come to recognize the value of unity they see in the papacy—with a redefined sense of office and mission—a sign of Christian unity.

This is not to say that the Catholic Church is perfect. Peter often found himself on the wrong side of the argument. This is not to say that Christ is not the head of the Church—indeed the entire Church is the body of Christ in the world today. But it is to acknowledge that Jesus established a community to carry his message and that he set up a structure in that community. That structure was passed along to the successors of the apostles long before the final Scripture was written let alone named Scripture. Jesus promised that the gates of hell would not prevail against that community headed by Peter or his successor. That is all that infallibility means, yet without that there is no guarantee that we today can encounter the true revelation of Jesus Christ.

1H. What is the revelation of Christianity?

So far our questions have concerned where we find God's revelation. Now we ask just what God has revealed. If we approach the Church to explore the message of Jesus, what will we be told?

First, Christians believe that God is personal, revealing himself in human history to draw closer to us and enter into relationship. Many ideas of God do not include the truth that God is personal. God could be thought of as simply a force, a law that governs and determines the universe. But that is not the Christian God. Our God wants to relate to us. And the story of his attempts to draw close is the story of revelation.

The Second Vatican Council describes our revelation as follows:

> In his goodness and wisdom God chose to reveal himself
> and to make known to us the hidden purpose of his will
> by which through Christ, the Word made flesh, man
> might in the Holy Spirit have access to the Father and
> come to share in the divine nature. Through this reve-
> lation, therefore, the invisible God speaks to men as

friends and lives among them, so that he may invite and take them into fellowship with himself.[16]

So revelation is God's communication to us, and as Christians we believe that this communication eventually took human form—Jesus.

But God's dealings with the human race began long before Jesus. At the dawn of history God revealed himself to a man and woman, Abraham and Sarah. He promised them a child even though they were old. From that promised child would spring a people who would receive God's blessing. God entered a covenant—a solemn agreement—with Abraham. And Abraham had faith in God and set out from his homeland to a new place.

Centuries later God appeared to Moses whose people were slaves in Egypt. God promised that he would free these slaves and lead them to a promised land. Through Moses God did indeed free the slaves and lead them through the Red Sea and out of the clutches of Pharaoh.

With each successive encounter we learn something more about God. We learn that he is a person. With Abraham and Sarah he is a God of blessing. With Moses and the people he is a liberator of slaves.

In the wilderness of Sinai, Moses received the law from God, establishing a covenant with Israel. Through the law Israel would be a model for all the nations: a sign of God's goodness and abundance. The law grounds Israel in the truth and the good; it establishes her on a solid foundation—God himself. It is a practical constitution. The law is Israel's most sacred possession, her sign of election by God for fulfilling his purpose in the world. While Christians believe that in Jesus the ritual parts of the law are superseded, we still hold to the ethical

---

16. De Revelatione 2.

teachings as fundamental to any humane society. These are summarized in the Ten Commandments.[17]

Later through the prophets these themes of blessing, liberation and law were amplified. Israel became like other nations; she desired wealth and power. The prophets called her to real justice in regard to her people. They spoke for the poor, giving voice to the oppressed and powerless. They called in God's name for an end to injustice, for compassion upon the poor, for a conversion to values which would put God first and work against human greed and the lust for power.[18] They cried out against Israel's arrogance. They castigated her lack of trust in God. They reminded her that her only claim to fame, her only hope lay in the Lord and his law.

When Israel fell to foreign conquerors the prophets offered words of consolation and hope: a day would come when once more Israel would be free. Indeed in that day the Messiah— God's anointed—would establish a reign of peace and justice in Israel that would flow forth to all the world.

Another tradition arose in Israel along with prophecy. It meditated upon God under the figure of Wisdom. Wisdom perceived God in his creation and the wise sought to find him there.[19] God was to be found too in human behavior. What is the way of the wise?[20] What is the good life?[21] What blessings come to the firstborn daughter of God,[22] who even descends to our earth and dwells among us?[23]

Christians believe that Jesus is that Messiah and God's Incarnate Wisdom. He proclaims the advent of the Kingdom of

---

17. Ex 20:1–17.
18. Am 5:7–13.
19. Jb 36:22—37:24.
20. Wis 6:1–12.
21. Sir 14:20—15:21.
22. Prv 3:13–35.
23. Prv 8:1–36.

God—a new society unlike any other—based upon God's love for us and founded upon healing and forgiveness. Through his preaching and parables Jesus describes the Kingdom. In his signs and miracles we glimpse the Kingdom breaking into our present world. And through his death and resurrection Jesus shows that God's love cannot be stopped even by death itself. Indeed Jesus so embodied his message that Christians believe he himself is the full revelation of God. He does not replace previous revelations; rather, as he himself says,[24] he brings revelation to fulfillment.

Since Jesus is the full revelation of God he is the end of revelation as well. Other people may have revelations from God; they may encounter God in mystical experiences. But these revelations are private. They do not add to what we have heard from Jesus. What he has revealed is not only God's love for all creatures but God's forgiveness and God's plan for bringing all creation home.

While Jesus has revealed the fullness of God to us, this does not imply that we have comprehended this revelation in its fullness. God's revelation is greater than any one person or age. Thus Christians continue to meditate upon and plumb the mysteries of God's revelaton. Out of this meditation have come the great Christian doctrines which do not add to the revelation but deepen our understanding of it.

That revelation has ended with Jesus does not mean that God's working in our history is over. We do not believe that once Jesus returned to his Father the two simply retired to await the outcome. God who made himself known to Moses because of his people's misery is still today involved in the struggle for liberation. God who forgave and healed in Jesus' ministry today carries on that same ministry of healing and forgiveness through Christians and the Church.

---

24. Mt 5:17–19.

For fundamentalists this exhausts revelation. The idea only applies to the specific revelation of God in the history of Israel and Christianity. They do not accept the idea of private revelation—that revelation of God to individuals—which Catholicism has room for.

Catholics go on to acknowledge other revelations besides that which founds our tradition. We see a natural revelation of God in creation itself. Humanity can come to know something of God through human reason. And we can acknowledge encounters with God in other religious traditions. The universal inclusiveness of Catholicism embraces truth wherever it is to be found and does not limit it to one particular instance even if that instance is the divine revelation of God himself.

1I. How reasonable is this revelation?

Since Christianity is a religion of salvation it is presumed that we are in need of saving. Things are not as they should be; this world is not all right simply the way it is. If it were, why would it even need a savior? There is something seriously wrong with the human condition and the world. As G.K. Chesterton once said, original sin (the Christian term for that condition) is the one Christian doctrine proclaimed everyday in newspaper headlines around the world.[25] What is the impact upon our thinking processes of this sinful condition?

Catholicism is optimistic. Yes, we are not what we were meant to be in God's eyes. Something is terribly wrong with the human race and with the world we have created. But there is something wonderful about us in our best moments as well: our art, literature, music, philosophy as well as our religions. There certainly is no exclusively Christian claim to the great moments and monuments of humanity. Plato has thought as deeply as

---

25. See question 2A.

any Christian. Hindu art has as many revelations of beauty as does Western Christian art.

Because we have fallen we cannot arrive at the full truths of revelations by our own reason and experience. There is no way we can achieve wholeness or salvation on our own. But reason allows us to perceive certain truths about the world and thus prepares us to receive the fullness of revelation from Jesus. Through reason we can discover the existence of God and certain things about God as well, such as that God is true, good, beautiful and one. All of these truths are part of natural revelation.

Of course human reason is not infallible. It can fall into error and often does. It is tinged with original sin like all else about us. But it is the creation of God himself and reflects God. And the fruits of human reason, namely the worldwide treasury of human achievement and civilization in all its infinite variety, are signs of the loving God who is the Creator of this reason. Indeed some say that reason provides our greatest likeness to God.

Reason does have its limits. It can tell us certain things about God but it cannot reveal God in all his glory. For that God must manifest himself in history, to Moses, to the prophets, and above all through Jesus. But what is revealed does not contradict or replace our reason. Rather it brings what we have discovered through reason to fulfillment and perfection. We could not experience God's saving love for us except through Jesus, but that revelation is consistent with what we have discovered about God on our own.

To say that revelation is not contradictory to reason does not mean that there is no place for mystery and paradox. Revelation surpasses our limited human reason. We cannot comprehend revelation—it will always remain a mystery because God is much greater than we are.

Reason can explore revelation and understand it better. This is the task of the theologian. Catholicism has always held a special but limited place for reason. Abelard and not Thomas Aquinas is the great rationalistic theologian. Thomas, following Aristotle, was more concerned with the evidence gathered from the external world and its relation to reason than with reason as a tool unto itself.

1J. Why are Catholic and Protestant bibles different?

There are really two questions implied here. First Protestants and Catholics have traditionally considered the Bible to have different contents or books. Then also there have been both Protestant and Catholic translations of the Scriptures. We will deal with the question of different contents to the Scripture first.

Versions
A hallmark of the Protestant-Catholic split has been the promotion of two different lists of books which make up the Bible. All Christians share a common New Testament: the Scriptures concerning Jesus. However a number of books in the Old Testament, accepted as Scripture by Catholics and Orthodox, are regarded as non-scriptural by Protestants. To see how these differences arose we will consider the growth of the Bible.

The Scriptures refer to a number of different writings gathered together to make up the Bible. These writings cover many centuries and include the Scriptures of Israel.

Ancient Israel drew up no official canon (list) of Scripture. Instead there were three groups of scriptural writings to which people referred. Most important were the five books of Moses called the law (torah). It includes the stories of Israel's birth and liberation as well as the many laws upon which she was

established by God. Second in importance were the writings of
the prophets. Indeed when Jesus refers to the law and the
prophets he is referring to the Scriptures. A final category were
called simply the writings: works of history (Chronicles), poetry
(Psalms and Job), instruction and wisdom (Proverbs and
Ecclesiastes). This group was not as well defined as the
collections of the law and the prophets. And the writings
continued to be added to in some communities up until the
time of Jesus.

While there was no official list there was a version of the
Scriptures common in the early Christian period. Hebrew was a
dead and largely unknown language. Jews were scattered
throughout the Greco-Roman world whose common language
was Greek. Thus, as the story goes, seventy Jewish scholars
gathered at Alexandria to produce a Greek translation of the
Holy Scriptures. This translation, known as the Septuagint (for
seventy), was the version most familiar to Jews throughout the
world at the beginning of the Christian era. It included all the
books in the present Old Testament plus a huge selection of
writings.

When the authors of the New Testament who wrote in Greek
quote the Hebrew Scriptures they quote not the original
Hebrew but the Greek Septuagint. So when Matthew describes
the virgin birth of Christ[26] he quotes Isaiah 7:14 as the
prophecy foreseeing this event. But the original Hebrew of
Isaiah had used the word "alma" which simply means a young
girl. However Matthew's Greek translation of this verse used
the word "parthenos" which means virgin—a meaning not
foreseen by the Hebrew original but which Matthew saw as
foretelling the virgin.

Only after the Christian era did Jewish scholars come together
and decide upon a list of books to be regarded as scriptural.
They made their criterion the book's availability in Hebrew.

---

26. Mt 1:18–25.

Those books no longer extant in Hebrew or originally composed in Greek or another language were excluded; these included a number of the writings.

Christians continued to use the Septuagint. And debate raged whether certain books should be regarded as Scripture. St. Jerome who produced the next great translation of the Scriptures into Latin (called the Vulgate) defined three categories of Old Testament books. First were those books which existed in Hebrew and were thus beyond question. Then came books existing only in Greek translations. Jerome called these deutero-canonical: a second list of books. Over these books there was some doubt. Finally there were a number of books which were definitely not to be regarded as Scripture although they had been included in the Septuagint. These Jerome called the apocrypha.

The New Testament is a different story. A number of writings circulated among the churches in the early days. There were Gospels, letters of apostles, books of discipline. And from these emerged some which Christians began to consider Sacred Scripture—on the same footing with the Old Testament Scriptures. The lists varied slightly between different communities. Certain books were above question such as the four Gospels and the letters of Paul. Others were debated. Eventually Christians agreed upon the current twenty-seven books of the New Testament.

So things stood until Martin Luther. He decided to take a second look at the canon of Scriptures. First he rejected the deutero-canonical books. Only those books found in Hebrew could be included. Thus Luther followed the Jewish criterion rather than common Christian practice. Then Luther wanted to examine the New Testament as well. He believed that justification by faith should be the criterion for selecting the books, and he had grave doubts about the Letter of James and some other New Testament books. But his disciple Melanchthon prevailed upon him to accept the traditional list of New Testament books, and there were no changes made. In answer to Luther the Roman Church drew up her own canon or list of the Old Testament following Jerome.

Actually the differences between the two lists of Scripture today are not all that crucial. Scripture scholars of both Catholic and Protestant backgrounds agree that the deutero-canonical Scriptures are not as central to our faith as are the other books. But they are quite valuable because of the glimpses afforded of Israel's development from the time of the last prophet until Jesus—information we would not otherwise have. For this they are indispensable. As in other questions of the Protestant Reformation agreement today results from advances of scholarship and a change of climate; we find sharing and consensus where before was only controversy and strife.

Translations
Unless you are fluent in Hebrew, Greek and assorted obscure languages such as Aramaic, you have to read the Scriptures in a translation. Let us take a short look at the modern history of biblical translation.

The Protestant Reformation produced two great translations. Martin Luther's helped create the modern German language, and the King James Version (hereafter referred to as KJV) has colored and shaped English with its style and familiar quotations ever since. For English peoples the KJV has long held sway as the most popular translation.

The KJV was a wonderful translation, and there is no denying its sheer beauty; indeed some parts far surpass the originals. But have scholars learned nothing important about the Bible in the last four hundred years? Can everyone be expected to read and understand a translation made at the time of Shakespeare?

In reaction to the KJV Catholics produced a translation taking its name from the French town where it was completed

(Catholics being exiled from England at the time). This Douai Version was later revised and called the Douai-Rheims Version. Unfortunately its language and translation are simply not on a par with the KJV—it is often awkward and stilted.

The twentieth century has seen a number of popular translations appear, and there is need of them. Biblical scholarship advanced by leaps and bounds in the nineteenth and twentieth centuries. We know more about the Scriptures today than at any other time since they were written. Further, the English language itself has changed. There is need for a contemporary translation.

One of the most popular modern translations is the most conservative. The Revised Standard Version (RSV) is actually a revision of the KJV in the light of modern scholarship and usage. Errors in the KJV have been corrected and archaic language updated. Whenever possible, however, the beauty of the older version has been kept intact. Thus the RSV has the advantage of the old familiarity and warmth of the KJV combined with the best of modern knowledge.

Roman Catholic scholars at the French biblical school in Jerusalem have produced a modern translation from the original languages and with extensive notes: the Jerusalem Bible. This popular translation now has an English version. The English is not a translation of the French, but goes back to the original languages. However in questionable passages the translators have followed the decisions of the French scholars.

Three distinguished translations have been completed by twentieth century British and American scholars. The New English Bible (NEB) is primarily a Protestant undertaking but Catholic scholars also served on the committee. In this country the New American Bible (NAB) is predominantly the work of Catholics although again Protestant scholars joined in the effort. Thus both translations are truly ecumenical. The differences concern style and the slight differences between

British and American English. Finally the American Bible
Society produced a new translation: Good News for Modern
Man. This translation using simple English strives for clarity
and simplicity, but does not have the literary quality of some
translations.

As can be seen the days of sectarian Bible translations are past.
Today Protestants and Catholics cooperate and share
scholarship between them. Thus the choice of a translation
depends upon other criteria.

Ask yourself what you want from the Bible. Do you want the
resonances of the English literary tradition? Then you might
choose the RSV. Are you more concerned with a new attempt
to do what the KJV did for its day? Then you would choose the
New English Bible which in its own right is a work of literary
beauty. Or select the Jerusalem Bible which included such
people as Tolkien (of Lord of the Rings fame) on its board of
translators. Is your primary interest clarity and good modern
scholarship? Then the New American Bible or Good News for
Modern Man might appeal to you.

Look over each to find which one best suits your interests and
needs. Use a verse such as John 3:16 as a test verse for
comparison. All these versions are accurate; all are wonderful
gifts to the Christian community.

There are also versions that are not strictly translations but
rather paraphrases. These can be very helpful, for the
Scriptures are not always easy to read and understand. But
remember when using a paraphrase that you are reading
someone's interpretation of Scripture rather than the original
text. And at least some paraphrases such as the Living Bible are
slanted toward a particular viewpoint.

Jesus Christ

2A. Why do we need a savior?

The savior is the dominant image of Jesus in our culture today. Why we are in need of saving? The Christian response to this question lies in the doctrine of original sin.[1]

We need not look very far in our world to meet up with real evil. If we take a rather optimistic view of things we may say that evil is only the result of mistakes, a lack of communication, or improper socialization and education. Now some evil is attributable to just such factors. But there is also conscious evil. Certainly there is need of a savior to right these evils if that be possible.

But looking even more closely at human activity we find a certain bias toward evil in humanity as a whole. St. Paul recognizes this propensity toward evil, and he describes it well.[2] He says that he may know that one thing is good and another evil. Yet even though he knows, he finds himself doing what is evil and unable to accomplish the good.

Most of the time we blind ourselves to what is really going on. We do not examine our motives carefully. We deceive ourselves into thinking that everything is all right. But Paul has no such illusions. He is not talking about man in the abstract. He is talking from experience about Paul. Why does he tend toward evil?

---

1. Met briefly before in question 11.
2. Rom 7:15–20.

47

Paul uses one of the Israelite stories of human origins to speak of his insight. Adam and Eve[3] were the first man and woman. They lived in the Garden of Eden where everything they needed was supplied. Only one condition was required: they must not eat of the tree of the knowledge of good and evil. The serpent in the garden tempted the woman with the forbidden fruit. She fell to temptation and persuaded the man to eat as well. When God discovered what had happened he expelled them from the garden, driving them into the cruel world where we have had to make our living ever since.

Scripture scholars consider this not history but a story of origins. There are elements in the story arising from Israel's current situation. For example, the serpent is the cursed animal who deceives the couple. The serpent cult was popular in Canaan and a religious threat to Israel. What better than to cast your rival in the enemy's role?

Paul retells the story to make his own point.[4] There is something seriously wrong with us. This defect does not come from God. It is not simply built into us. It comes from some original fall from grace, some refusal to cooperate with God that has become hereditary. It is now part of our make-up. Original sin states that left to our own devices we will sooner or later succumb to evil.

St. Augustine shared a wonderful story of the presence of this sinful condition in his own life. He reflected back to his youth to a day when he and some friends stole some pears, and asked: Why did we do this sinful thing? It was not because we were hungry. We were not. It wasn't because we had a great craving for pears. In fact the pears were not even ripe. Rather we took joy in the simple act of doing wrong. We knew it was wrong to rob, yet we did it with relish. Each of us shares that propensity to sin as part of our human heritage.

---

3. Gn 2:5—3:24.
4. Rom 5–8.

We need a savior first of all to heal the sin in our world as well as the condition that leads us into sin. But that sin has consequences as well. There is fear. We know we have done wrong. We know we are not all right. Fear consumes us. Often our fear is ultimately directed toward God. He will punish us. He will be angry. But for most our fear is generalized. We are simply afraid—and we could use a savior from our fear.

Sin produces guilt as well. When Adam and Eve saw what they had done, they saw their nakedness and were ashamed, covering themselves with fig leaves. We share those feelings of guilt. Psychiatry is consumed with the task of lifting guilt. Often guilt is quite out of proportion to our sin. We need salvation from guilt.

The story says that death was a penalty of this original sin. Certainly death hangs like a sword over our lives threatening to cut us off from all we hold dear. Often the threat of death prevents people from living. Can anyone save us from this sin, this fear, this guilt, this death? We greatly need a savior!

2B. Do Christians believe that Jesus Christ is the savior?

Christians certainly believe that Jesus saves us. But the issue is what salvation really means. Some understand it as meaning that Jesus saves us from the fires of hell. Unfortunately too much Christian thought has been along these lines and the original meaning of salvation has been lost. The word comes from the Latin word "salus" which means "health." To be saved means to be made healthy, to be made whole.

We might consider original sin as incompleteness: something about us is not what God intended. Our efforts to succeed lead to failure. Jesus shows us the way to health and wholeness. And his emptying of himself in death shows us the way to eternal life and is our promise that we too shall enjoy eternal life through him. Our lives are changed: the way we see things, our values, our feelings, our purpose for living.

How does Jesus save us and make us whole? He preaches the Kingdom of God—a condition quite different from the world we are used to. In the Kingdom we discover a loving Father who seeks us out and wants to bring us home to him. We discover that some of the things we took most seriously are really not too important; Jesus weans us from activities like worry, fear, judgment. He asks us to look closely at our anger, righteousness and pride. He encourages us to be forgiving and shows how God has already extended his forgiveness to us. He calls on God to heal people of their illnesses and encourages us to do likewise. He teaches us through parables and teachings to recognize the lies of the world and begin to move more and more into God's Kingdom.

He recognizes how fear of death prevents us from living fully. So Jesus takes on this death. He goes to Jerusalem, places himself within the power of the church and state and is condemned to death. The disciples are frightened and confused. They scatter in fear. But on the third day Jesus appears to them. Yes, he really died. But, more important, he is alive now in a new way. His Father has raised him from the grave into everlasting life and happiness. Jesus offers that same generous gift to us. We do not need to heal ourselves or save ourselves. We cannot do so anyway. In Jesus is the power to heal and make us whole. All we need do is surrender to him.

Thus the Christian believes in a better way of life which is the Kingdom of God. He or she has seen that better way in Jesus and in his followers. In becoming a Christian we surrender to Jesus, confident that he will eventually bring us beyond death into fullness of life in his Father's Kingdom. Meanwhile we have enlisted on the side of the Kingdom. We attempt through our prayer, study and work to become more and more citizens of the Kingdom. We live in this world as signs of the Kingdom's presence. We engage in Jesus' ministry: healing sickness, forgiving sins, freeing prisoners. We ourselves are healed, forgiven and freed through our contact with Jesus in the Christian community. We have no ultimate allegiance to the present world and state of things. Instead we look forward to the day when this age will pass away and the Kingdom will come in its fullness. In the meantime we are in the world but not of it.

2C. Are the Gospels accurate biographies of Jesus?

There is something wrong with this often asked question. It presumes that the Gospels intend to be biographies. But do they? The word means good news. And the Gospels are primarily proclamations of that good news through telling the stories of and about Jesus.

Even if the Gospels are not biographies, can we presume that what they say about Jesus is literally true? The Last Supper is the Passover in the Synoptic Gospels,[5] while in John Jesus dies as the Passover lamb is being slain.[6] Jesus also seems to contradict himself—at one time he says that whoever is not against him is for him,[7] and at another time he says that whoever is not for him is against him.[8] How do we reconcile these two statements?

Let us look at the way scholars believe the Gospels came to be written. We start with Jesus and his disciples. They were together for a period of time during which Jesus told parables, taught them, and performed many signs.

After Easter when the disciples were sent with the good news out into the world, they took with them as precious treasures

---

5. Mt 26:17 and parallels.
6. Jn 19:31.
7. Mk 9:40.
8. Mt 12:30.

these stories both of and about Jesus. When they told people about Jesus they shared the stories. As Christian communities formed they preserved these stories and sayings among themselves. They would meditate and reflect upon them and hand them on to new or young Christians. After a number of years, someone got the brilliant idea of writing down these stories. And the Gospel of Mark is born.

The Gospel of Mark may have gone through other stages of composition before assuming its current shape. But Mark created the Gospel format: using the different stories to proclaim the good news of Jesus. And since for the early Christians the overwhelming good news was Jesus' triumph over death in the resurrection, almost half of Mark's Gospel is taken up with the story of Jesus' death and resurrection which probably took concrete form long before. The parables and stories of the first part of his Gospel almost seem a prologue to the real story.

But Mark does not intend to write a modern historically accurate account of Jesus. Mark is concerned with the good news. And he does not believe that Jesus' words and deeds are things of the past. They are alive and life-giving today. So Mark and the other Gospel writers after him will change the original words or their context to allow Jesus to address events and situations in the contemporary community.

Many parables have a number of layers like an archeological dig. The first layer is the original parable of Jesus. And sometimes this is extremely hard to construct from the final Gospel account. Then there are meanings and associations that the parable picked up as it was handed down through the various Christian communities. Finally there may be a new interpretation that the author brings out in his work.

For an example of this layering, look at the parable of the sower and the seed.[9] There is the original parable, then an

9. Mt 13:1–23.

allegorization, and finally Matthew's application of the parable to his own church. The Gospel writers were not distorting or betraying Jesus in this endeavor. Rather they feel that Jesus' words are living words able to address new situations, and they have the confidence that Jesus' stories speak as directly to the new listeners as to their original audience. Of course such practice plays havoc with modern attempts to discover just what Jesus originally said. But we can't blame the Gospel writers for not answering the questions we want answered.

Catholics believe that the Gospels provide a true picture of Jesus. But before we can say that the individual details are historically accurate we must discover just what the original author intended to communicate. And we must attempt to trace that story from its place in a certain Gospel back through the oral tradition to Jesus himself. This of course is work for biblical scholars rather than lay people.

This need for scholarship does not reserve the Bible to scholars. We can and should read the Bible not to determine historical accuracy but to hear the good news. Scripture is a living word. When we read Scripture our primary concern is not what Jesus originally said to whom, but what Jesus has to say to our condition today.

When Jesus scolds the unbelievers we learn nothing if we act superior, believing that he is addressing only the Jews of his day. No, he is talking to the unbelieving part of us. When we read the Gospels he is talking not to Bartamaeus or Lazarus, Mary and Martha. His original words may have been addressed to them but the living Word transcends that original conversation to address us. Jesus talks to human beings; if we are human his words find their mark in us. Whether they are the exact words originally spoken is not the issue. They are words alive with good news words that transform us.

2D. What does Jesus teach?

For some Christians the teachings and works of Jesus take
second place to the idea of the Christ or Savior. This results
from over-emphasis upon Paul. Jesus' earthly life, ministry and
teachings are as important as his death and resurrection. And
they are necessary in appreciating the death and resurrection.

Jesus is a Jew. He sees himself not as the replacement of God's
revelation to Israel but rather as the fulfillment, perfection or
completion of that revelation.[10] We cannot hope to understand
Jesus except in the context of Israel. Indeed catholicism sees
itself as the continuation of Israel. Christian hatred of Jews
perverts Jesus' teaching.[11]

Jesus' message is summarized in the statement: "Repent, for the
Kingdom of God is at hand."[12] The Kingdom of God is the
focus of Israel's faith—a main theme throughout the Old
Testament.[13] Liberation is the first characteristic of the
Kingdom. And the work of God in this world continues to be
the liberation of peoples—a central Christian ministry. The idea
that Christianity only has to do with another world or a future
life is a distortion of revelation. Judaism and Christianity are at
root political, concerned with human society and relationships.

In the context of Israel's history Jesus does not so much add to
that history; rather he brings a wholeness not before realized.
He turns the focus inward. Whereas before the emphasis is
upon exterior actions and relationships—do not steal, do not
cheat the poor, do not commit adultery—Jesus interiorizes to
get at the root of our feelings and actions.[14]

---

10. Mt 5:17–19.
11. See questions 3F and 5J.
12. Mk 1:15.
13. See question 1H.
14. Mt 15:10–20.

Jesus draws attention to emotions and feelings underlying and giving rise to actions. He talks about fear, judgment, worry, anger, pride, envy. And he shows how we can cease to be dominated by these feelings and move toward real happiness.

God is not vindictive but rather forgiving. And Jesus invites us to be forgiving as well in order to experience the peace that forgiveness brings. He is compassionate toward others—healing their sickness, forgiving their sins, feeding their hungers. So he reveals the true face of God. If we would act more like God, Jesus suggests that we would find our lives richer and happier.[15]

And what is this face of God that Jesus reveals? It is the face of love. And while it is definitely untrue that the God of the Old Testament doesn't show this face of love and compassion,[16] nevertheless Jesus makes love primary as never before.

Jesus reveals the interior dimension of the Kingdom. But he does more. He proclaims that the Kingdom is at hand. We can experience this Kingdom in our lives today. And repeatedly through his ministry people are drawn into the Kingdom, their lives transformed.

Consider Zacchaeus the tax collector, a stingy, perverse, wretch if ever there was one.[17] Jesus doesn't scold or tell Zacchaeus that he must change his ways. Instead he tells this friendless man that he wants to stay with him—to become Zacchaeus' friend. What a difference that offer of friendship makes! Zacchaeus spontaneously declares that he will give half his money to the poor and will pay back anything illegally acquired. And he says it with such happiness that he must have moved into the Kingdom.

---

15. Mt 5:48.
16. Read Hosea or Jeremiah.
17. Lk 19:1–10.

The best description of Jesus' ministry is the passage he chooses himself from Isaiah:

> The spirit of the Lord is upon me
> for he has anointed me.
> He has sent me to bring the good news to the poor,
> to proclaim liberty to captives
> and to the blind new sight,
> to set the downtrodden free,
> to proclaim the Lord's year of favor.[18]

The God of Jesus is a God of liberation, healing, forgiveness, joy and compassion. And we come to know this God whom Jesus calls "Daddy" (Abba) through Jesus's life and ministry.[19]

2E. Did Jesus die for our sins?

Here is the very core of our faith. The difference between catholic and fundamentalist is not so much disagreement concerning fundamentals as the way those fundamental beliefs are understood in the overall context. Both accept the word for this Christian doctrine—the atonement.

But "atonement" is double-barreled. Originally it comes from the Old English and reflects its components: at-one-ment. By the atonement Jesus makes us one again with God. This is the Catholic understanding.

But the word can also be taken as meaning "appeasement." God is angry at our sin. So Jesus, the totally perfect human being, by his death on the cross appeases God who ceases to be angry with us.

---

18. Is 40:3–5; Lk 3:4–6.
19. Mk 14:36; Rom 8:15; Gal 4:6.

Paul declares that God was in Christ reconciling the world to himself.[20] This reconciliation was effected in Jesus' suffering and death on the cross. From a Christian perspective humanity is defective—we have a tendency toward sin.[21] All our attempts to overcome that sinful tendency meet with failure and often create greater sin and misery. Looking closely at the human condition, freed from the blinkers we use to deceive ourselves, we cry out with Paul, "Who will save us?"[22]

Through Jesus we are made whole and reconciled with God. One of the earliest and most beautiful images of this reconciliation is found in an early Christian hymn.[23] Although Jesus was divine he did not cling to his divinity. Instead he emptied himself and took on our human condition, even to the point of experiencing our death, and on a cross at that. How much God loves us! He reaches out, emptying himself of his divinity to put on our humanity and seek us out.

And what kind of a life does he live? A life of obedience, even to death. Original sin is often described as a sin of disobedience. Our lives are examples of disobedience—we may know the truth and what is good, yet something within us balks at following the way of truth, especially if that way looks as though it might lead to death of any kind.

Jesus' action of emptying himself reveals a different way of living. We attempt to become full of ourselves. We want to be in the center of things. We would like to be the God of the universe, and if we were, by God, we would cling to it. Yet what does God do? He empties himself of his glory, taking on our condition. Jesus points toward real wholeness and reconciliation. Fulfillment lies in truly becoming who we indeed

---

20. 2 Cor 5:19.
21. See question 2A.
22. Rom 7:24.
23. Phil 2:6–11.

are—human beings obedient to our condition rather than people scrambling to become something we are not.

When Jesus accepts the human condition, even death, what happens? God raises him high, giving him a name above all others. Jesus is proclaimed Lord of all creation. He brings us home to our Father. And we see that if we too will follow the way of Jesus—of being obedient to the human condition, of learning to live humanely through his teachings and example, of accepting even death as part of who we are—then we too will be raised up in Jesus to enjoy eternal life.

This wonderful hymn presents a very different image from the wrathful God demanding human sacrifice. Yes, Jesus dies to take away our sins. But it is not a death demanded by a cruel God. Rather Jesus himself is the expression of God's love who comes to seek us out even while we are in sin. And that love does not shirk death to show us that death is not ultimate and that it cannot really harm us. Jesus takes the sting out of death, snatching victory from the mouth of the grave.[24] We need no longer live in fear. The battle is won; victory is ours in Jesus Christ.[25]

2F. Do Catholics believe that doing good works can win one's salvation?

A major issue of the Protestant Reformation centered on the place of good works in a Christian's life. Some consider Christianity to be a religion in which people are judged according to what they have done in their lives. But such an idea ignores the reality that we cannot make ourselves whole, that we cannot save ourselves. And the good news is that we need not try to save ourselves. God has reached out to us, reconciling us through Jesus' death on the cross.

---

24. 1 Cor 15:55.
25. See also Question 3F.

In Luther's time Catholicism had degenerated into a works theology which Luther, being a committed Catholic, took seriously, much to his misery. He was constantly in a quandary about his salvation. In his eyes all his imperfections stood in the way of his salvation.

His insight recaptured the primacy of faith. We cannot make ourselves whole or perfect. But through faith in Christ Jesus we are justified in God's eyes.[26] In Christ God chooses to see us not as the miserable failures we seem to be in our own and one another's eyes but rather the glorious human beings we are meant to become in Christ Jesus. Here Luther and Catholics are in agreement, now that the dust of argument and strife has settled.

We are justified by faith, not by works. But how does the person of faith live? When we encounter Jesus we convert to a new set of values and life. Our old life is dead and now the reality of the Spirit guides us. Thus Christians will act charitably. It is not that we will not make mistakes and sin. We are still human—still, as Luther said, sinner as well as reconciled. But we will in faith attempt to act according to the light of Christ rather than the values of the world. Again, now that the controversy is past, Protestants and Catholics can agree. Christians by their very nature, which is at core Christ, naturally do good works.

Now there are various problems that we can get into because of this distinction. Often Christians try to put the cart before the horse. We attempt to do good works before we have allowed the reality of Christ into our lives fully. We are still trying to perfect ourselves—to be good. But the first and most important step is to allow the reality of God's love to transform us.

When we try to do good without being motivated by the love of Christ, we tend to take burdens upon ourselves which are not

---

26. Gal 3:6.

truly ours. And we set ourselves up for failure. Mother Teresa of Calcutta in her community insures that her people get things right. All persons joining the community spend the initial time in prayer. And the content of their meditation is God's love for them. Only when they are so full of God's love that they cannot contain it do they go out into the world and share that love with the poor. And as soon as they feel a depletion of God's love within them, they are to drop whatever work they are doing and retreat into prayer again.

For good works flow from God. They are not our doing. They are not our responsibility; it is God's work and responsibility. We are mere instruments of his work. Too often we want to get on with the work before we are really ready for it. And then the work is poisoned with our egos, our sinfulness, our pride. When the work fails we feel we have failed. And when the work succeeds we feel we have done it.

We are saved not by what we do but rather by Jesus Christ. But there is also a danger of making faith itself into a work. Some say that if you do not have faith in Jesus you are going to hell. Now isn't this faith then an action, a work which the person must do in order to achieve salvation?

A real Christian knows that God has done all the work. He has already reconciled the world in Jesus Christ. There is nothing left to be done. He invites us to discover this good news and join in the celebration. But to think that your act of faith will save you is just as wrong as thinking that your act of charity will save you. Jesus Christ has saved us all—not just those who do the proper thing whether it be an act of faith or a good work. He died to save sinners—and there are no distinctions between worthy and unworthy sinners.

2G. Did Jesus really rise from the dead?

The resurrection forms the center of our faith. Although Jesus actually died and was buried, on the third day we believe that his body disappeared from the tomb and Jesus appeared to his disciples and others. He is no longer dead. As the early Christians said, he was raised up to new life by his Father.[27] This new life is not of a ghost or a spirit. The risen Jesus has a body similar to his earthly body but now glorified.

All orthodox Christians share this belief in Jesus' bodily resurrection. The New Testament attests it universally. Paul puts the question bluntly as usual: if Christ did not rise from the dead, then our faith is in vain.[28] Jesus' resurrection is the great breakthrough of the Kingdom into our world.

Resurrection was a concept popular among certain groups in Jesus' day. It formed part of the apocalyptic tradition: on the day of the Lord, the dead would be raised up to participate in the Kingdom which would replace the present age. The original witnesses of the resurrection interpreted it as the confirming sign that the Kingdom had dawned. Jesus is the first fruits of those to be raised from the dead.[29] By Jesus' death the present age has passed away. His resurrection inaugurates the Kingdom. The early Christians expected a quick end of the world so that Christ might establish his Kingdom.

That the world did not end provoked a major crisis in the early Church. Christians began to reinterpret and leave behind the apocalyptic thought in which the original message had been couched. As Christianity entered the Greco-Roman world, resurrection received other nuances and emphases. These

---

27. Acts 2:32–33; 1 Cor 15:3–8.
28. 1 Cor 15:12–19.
29. 1 Cor 15:20.

resonances became part of our Christian understanding of the resurrection.

And indeed we look forward to profounder insight into the resurrection, as our faith encounters other cultures and spiritual traditions. We do not need to cling to a narrow revelation that might not speak well to our own time. Our faith lives and God communicates through our own time and ideas. It does not lift us out of our age; it helps us understand the deeper truths in the light of our age.

Some interpret the resurrection narratives literally. But examining the resurrection stories closely, details differ from one story to another. For example, Jesus tells Mary not to cling to him because he has not yet ascended to his Father.[30] This implies that his body is material and can be clung to. Yet in another story Jesus walks through a wall.[31]

Taken literally these stories work us into a corner, and we must heap explanation upon explanation to make everything harmonize.

The resurrection surpasses our attempts to fully understand it. The stories point toward a reality they cannot fully describe. To take them literally demeans the reality they seek to communicate.

The resurrection is much more than the greatest miracle of Jesus; in the resurrection the Kingdom breaks through. Jesus is no longer confined to space and time. It is not necessary to have been in Galilee at the turn of the era to meet and know Jesus. He is alive today. He is present among his people—indeed the Church herself forms the body of Christ.[32] Through his

---

30. Jn 20:17.
31. Jn 20:19–20.
32. See question 3B.

resurrection Jesus maintains a concrete presence throughout time and space.

Nor is the event of the resurrection limited to one time and place. Yes, Jesus did indeed rise victorious over death on a certain day. But that triumph continues to break into history and to be communicated to all people. And that communication happens in a number of ways but primarily in the celebration of Easter—the feast of the resurrection.

Each year late on the night before Easter we gather in darkness for the lighting of the new fire—a symbol of Christ bringing light into our darkness. We listen to the great stories of our faith. Then those to be baptized come forward. They are plunged under the waters, joining Jesus in his death, and as they are raised up, we in these new Christians witness the reality of Jesus' resurrection.

Resurrection is not simply an event that happened to Jesus. He shares it with all who follow him. And the mystery of resurrection—that for every death there is the hope of resurrection—lies at the center of being a Christian. Jesus' resurrection gives deepest meaning to the way we live our lives. At Easter and particularly in baptism we experience the reality of resurrection.

But how can we understand the resurrection? It is not an event simply seen by those original witnesses. It is not like a car accident—if you are there you see it. For one thing Jesus was usually not seen by those who had no belief in him.[33]

Those who witness the risen Lord are already disciples and followers. And even they do not at first recognize Jesus—he is the same but different: glorified. Faith is needed to perceive the risen Lord. The disciples can't be called credulous

---

33. Paul seems to be the exception that proves the rule.

witnesses. After Jesus' death they are dead themselves, their
dreams crushed. And in each resurrection story Jesus or the
angels call these people back to their faith, back to life. He is
not dead; he is alive. Only when their faith has been quickened
do they see the resurrection.

We too must approach the resurrection with the eyes of faith.
Gradually as we come to trust Jesus our eyes are opened to the
reality of resurrection not just in Jesus' life but in our own as
well. We have been buried and raised with him in baptism. In
some small way the resurrection is working in our lives and
world to bring about God's Kingdom in its fullness. Our faith
reveals the reality of the resurrection which in turn deepens
and enriches our faith.

Finally there is an element of each resurrection story crucial to
it and not emphasized sufficiently. Each time Jesus is
discovered alive the person is sent out with this good news to
the world. As witnesses of Jesus' resurrection we are in turn
called to witness to others the reality of the resurrection. We are
not so much concerned with our own salvation and happiness.
Rather we hear Jesus' call to be his witnesses to the power of the
resurrection over death and the dawning of the Kingdom.

2H. Is Jesus really God? And if so, just how human can he be?

No orthodox Christian denies that Jesus is both fully divine and
fully human. Still many in their concrete working out of
Christianity lose the balance. Jesus either becomes simply a
great man or an inhuman God with all the answers to every
possible question.

The dogma of the incarnation, flowering from the stories of the
virgin birth and hammered out in the early councils,[34] declares

---

34. See question 1E.

that Jesus is fully human with no detriment to his divinity and fully divine with no detriment to his humanity. It is not enough to say that Jesus is a man divinely inspired with the word of God. No, he is God as the later Church affirmed. But on the other hand to believe that Jesus is a walking, talking, omniscient (although perhaps not omnipotent) divinity with the last word on every issue is to deny his true humanity, for humans by definition are finite and limited. The doctrine simply states that we cannot be true Christians if we focus upon one element to the neglect of the other.

And what of the picture of Jesus in the New Testament? First, the entire New Testament was written after the first Easter and through the new vision that Easter supplied. The Gospels do not provide an accurate and literal account of Jesus' activities and words.[35] They awaken faith in Jesus as the Lord of life.

In the Gospels the light of Easter shines back throughout the earlier ministry, coloring it. Even so, with one exception in John (which is a case unto itself), Jesus never claims that he is God. This would have been unthinkable and scandalous for a monotheistic Jew. The testimony to Jesus' divinity comes from the disciples' reflection on his teachings and ministry in the light of the resurrection.

Later councils would define Jesus as God from before his conception. He is the second person of the Trinity, not created like the rest of creation but birthed by the Father. Thus at no moment in Jesus' life is he not divine. He was not adopted by God at some point in his life.

But Jesus is also a full human being. And in recent years Catholics and others have begun again to meditate upon Jesus' human knowledge. Some Christians imagine Jesus lying in the manger with the entire plan of salvation in his mind. His life simply unfolds that plan. But how human would this Jesus be?

---

35. See question 2C.

Is not our ignorance, doubt, and fear vital to our humanity? Do we not come to knowledge by grappling with our life, through experience and testing? And could not Jesus come to knowledge the same way? Does it bring Jesus closer to believe that he always knew he would be resurrected in three days? Such knowledge would make it easy to endure the agonies of Calvary. Rather did he not simply trust God would bring him through? This is how we must face our own death. In such a light would not his faith in the Father be so much more a gift—coming as it did from a fully human condition of limitation and ignorance—than if his resurrection were certain knowledge?

Heresy is the attempt to settle for a part rather than a whole. It is easier to believe that Jesus is only God; then he can tell us exactly what to do and we have no choice but to obey and comply. This puts a new law in place of the old law. Or we could make Jesus simply human, and we would not have to contend with the mystery of his person—for elements about him are more than human. Each conclusion is heresy.

Christianity in its fullness makes us wrestle with a Jesus fully human yet fully divine. Only by keeping these two poles in tension do we meet the living Christ who is able to share our condition, our fears, our joys, our hopes, our disappointments, our insecurity, and our achievements. Only the living Christ who constantly eludes our attempts to fully understand him can really save us and make us whole.

2I. Do Christians expect Jesus to return to earth again?

Jesus lived in troubled, unsettling times. His homeland was occupied by Roman troops and before that repeatedly occupied by foreign powers, first Babylon, then Alexandrian Greece. There was much talk about the end of the world in Israel. And

a literature sounded these themes which are found in the Book
of Revelation as well as other places in Scripture.

Jesus announced that the Kingdom of God was at hand.[36] He
understood his mission as inaugurating the Kingdom which
would soon come with power and glory. Then the earthly
powers would be overturned and God would establish his own
reign over the world's peoples. On that day Israel looked
forward to all peoples turning to her and her God. The blind
would be given sight, the lame would walk, the poor would hear
the good news[37] and all tears would be wiped away as everyone
sat down at the great banquet of the Kingdom.[38] Jesus' signs
and miracles witnessed that the Kingdom was already breaking
into this world.

Jesus believed that the present state of things was not to last
long.[39] Perhaps he believed that the Kingdom would come with
power soon after his ministry. Certainly his disciples
understood him this way. There was a saying[40] that some of the
original disciples would still be alive when the Kingdom arrived.
We say that Jesus might have thought this way rather than that
he did. As modern Scripture scholarship makes clear, not every
word in Jesus' mouth in the Gospels is an actual word he said.

Certainly the early Christians believed that there was not much
time left before the Kingdom's glory would come. Paul advises
people not to marry[41]—what good will it do if it will all soon be
over? But as the years passed the world did not end. The
original disciples began to die. And Christians had to ask

---

36. Mk 1:15.
37. Lk 3:4–6.
38. Is 25:6–12.
39. Mk 13:1–2.
40. Mk 13:30.
41. 1 Cor 7:1–9.

whether there might be a longer time than expected between Easter and the end.

Some scholars understand Luke's work as an attempt to find a new perspective. The earliest Christians understood Jesus' resurrection as the first great event of the Kingdom's coming. He is the firstborn of the dead, and soon the others will join him. The cross signaled the end of this world's history and the beginning of the reign of God.

But Luke sees the cross not at the end of history but rather in the middle. He looks back at the long preparation for the Messiah and then forward to see the Church transforming history. Thus Luke does not simply write a Gospel but also a history of the early Church in which the ministry of Jesus is carried on by his disciples. In this twofold book the cross and resurrection are literally in the center rather than at the end as in Mark's Gospel.

Slowly Christians realized that the world would not end soon. New ways of understanding Jesus and his work arose, divorced from an immediate preparation for the end of the world. Today catholics are not overly concerned about the end of the world, at least in the non-nuclear sense. We have taken the work of Luke to heart, putting it central to our understanding of Jesus and his mission. We see history as a gradual growth of the Kingdom here in the world. The Church is a sign of the Kingdom to people today. Our struggle for peace and justice is part of the struggle of the Kingdom.

But while the return of Jesus may not be on our minds it remains a part of orthodox Christian thinking. We do not believe that things will simply go on forever. There is a meaning to history—especially Christian history. In Jesus God reveals the fullness of his Kingdom. The Holy Spirit makes us workers for that Kingdom. The Kingdom is struggling with the forces of this world. At times the world seems to win. At times the Kingdom glimmers. And at times the tension and struggle intensify.

While we may become curious about God's plan for us we receive no help from Jesus. He told his disciples neither the time nor the hour.[42] Instead he commands vigilance, watching the signs of the times.[43]

The Christian attitude toward Jesus' return holds to the virtue of hope. History is ultimately in God's hands. When things go badly for us, when evil seems to be winning, we have the hope (the same as those early Christians suffering Roman persecution) that at least at the end we shall see Jesus again. Then all will be made clear, every tear will be wiped away, and all will go into the banquet with great rejoicing. This belief gives us courage to continue working here and now, doing our small part to prepare the way of the Lord. To claim to know more is pure arrogance and probably demonic.

Apocalypse adds a healthy dimension to our Christianity. We might be tempted to think with this great span of time between the resurrection and the day of the Lord that the coming of the Kingdom has been placed in our hands. We have a great work to do. And we must struggle for the Kingdom. Now it is true that Christians should be about the task of preparing the way of the Kingdom and announcing the Kingdom's advent.

But the Kingdom's coming in no way depends upon us. God is bringing his Kingdom into our world. The Kingdom is an act of God that in no way depends upon what we do. Christianity is the proclamation of the great work God is accomplishing through Christ. To hear of that work allows us to join in solidarity with it. We can aid through living God's will—but the

42. Mk 13:32.
43. Mt 24:42–44.

coming or delaying of the work does not depend upon us but upon God who alone knows the time and the hour of his Kingdom's arrival.

2J. Is it possible to meet the living Christ today?

For Christians Jesus is not simply an historical figure. He is the living God, as much alive today as when he walked the earth. And Christians believe that they can encounter Jesus and be transformed by him today just as in his earthly ministry.

The primary way in which people meet the living Lord is through the Church. In Jesus God put on a human body and addressed us not from on high but rather as one of us. We continue to find God in our humanity.

Jesus tells his disciples that he will be present whenever two or three are gathered in his name.[44] Paul calls the Church the body of Christ.[45] And the message of Jesus which came among us in human form continues to do so through his followers. In the context of Christian community a person approaches Scripture. The community shows how to encounter Jesus in Scripture—it is not something that happens automatically. As the eunuch[46] said to Philip: How will I know about God unless someone explains it to me?

Catholics discover the living Lord through our worship together. The community assembles to pray and praise the Lord. Already we have the assurance that Jesus is with us in this prayer. Indeed our prayer is through Jesus—he will bring our concerns to the Father.

---

44. Mt 18:20.
45. 1 Cor 12:27.
46. Acts 8:26–40.

There are many ways to encounter Jesus today. We do this
primarily through the Christian community where Jesus is
constantly present. And in that community, especially at
worship, the presence of Christ bursts into our lives—through
Christian fellowship with one another, through the priest who
re-enacts the actions of Jesus, through the word of God in
Scripture and especially in the Gospel, through the action of
the Eucharist—receiving, thanking, breaking and
communing—and through the bread and wine themselves—the
body and blood of Jesus Christ.[47] Here Jesus is indeed present
in word and action, flesh and blood.

---

47. See question 4C.

The Church

3A. Who is the Holy Spirit?

The Holy Spirit is the forgotten aspect of Christianity. While
Christians certainly believe in the Holy Spirit, the reality of the
Spirit in Christian life has often been neglected. The Holy
Spirit is the third person of the Trinity: the love between the
Father and the Son. And the Spirit dwells in us, bringing us
home to the Father.

Toward the end, John's Gospel[1] questions why Jesus is
abandoning the disciples. Wouldn't it be better for him to
remain on earth to continue teaching and leading us? But Jesus
does not consider that the best course. He feels it necessary to
return to his Father. However he will not leave his followers
without help. He will send the Spirit, the Advocate, to lead us in
the truth.

We receive the gift of the Holy Spirit when we become
Christians. The Spirit is God dwelling in us. The Spirit brings
us wisdom and understanding, right judgment and courage,
knowledge and reverence, and wonder and awe in God's
presence.[2]

There has always been a tension between the Spirit within each
person and the unity of the community. For the Spirit blows
where it will.[3] It cannot be tied down. Yet Churches and

---

1. Jn 13:36–38; Jn 16:4–8.
2. Prayer at confirmation.
3. Jn 3:8.

institutions need roots and stability. Church history bears witness to this tension.

This tension is not bad, but it does make Christians, and Church leaders in particular, uncomfortable. Things cannot be as cut and dried as we might like. At her best the Church struggles with this tension. Whenever the individual is over-emphasized the community splits into tiny factions—each having its kernel of truth but missing the forest for the trees. When the institution gains the upper hand faith becomes moribund, fossilized in conformity rather than true unity.

The Holy Spirit dwells in each Christian. But for that very reason the Holy Spirit dwells in the Christian community as a whole. There is but one Spirit, so no real conflict between individuals and communities is possible. If I as an individual feel that the Spirit is telling me one thing but the Church as a whole does not feel that this is of the Spirit, conflict results.[4] The institution might use its power to silence the individual. But if the individual's ideas are of the true Spirit, they will prevail in the end. Living through such situations tests and deepens our faith.

The Holy Spirit which is poured upon us in baptism and confirmation is to be our comforter and guide on our Christian journey. The Spirit sanctifies us, heals us, teaches us, quickens us. The Spirit, if we cooperate, makes us divine.

Unfortunately much Christianity stops with half the revelation of Jesus—that he is the Christ. He is utterly different from us. So we put him on an altar and worship him, hoping that he will save us. If we have really missed the good news, we even believe that our salvation depends upon our being good rather than upon Jesus' cross and resurrection. Such an understanding of Christianity has little room for the Holy Spirit unless as a guide for the leaders or the Church as a whole.

---

4. See question 4G.

But such an understanding is only half of the good news. St. Athanasius put it best when he said: "In Jesus God became man so that through Jesus man might become God." Jesus shows us the way to divinity. He responds to our primordial yearning, present in the story of Adam and Eve: we want to become like God. And all of our civilization and culture is our attempt to achieve this goal.

Jesus makes it possible for us to become divinized. But it is not the way we think it is. It is not through seizing and grasping but through emptying and obedience.[5] And he gives us the gift of the Holy Spirit to lead us home to the Father. The Holy Spirit transforms us—he makes us divine.

The Holy Spirit gives Peter and John the power to carry on Jesus' ministry of healing.[6] The Holy Spirit allows Paul to carry the Gospel all the way to Rome. The Holy Spirit makes possible the great love and works of the saints. And that same Holy Spirit is given to us to transform us and bring us home, making us into Christ.

When the Holy Spirit is unleashed, wonderful and awesome things happen. We risk. We go where we have not been before. We conquer fear and sickness. We look death in the face and see that the joke is on death. Poor death will die. When we accept and trust in the Holy Spirit Jesus has sent us, miracles happen.

There will on occasion arise tension between the individual and the institution. Such tension is often the concrete work of our redemption. What we call the Spirit may be the voice of our own ego. And what the Church calls the Spirit may be the clerical or mass ego writ large. The Spirit manifests through the confrontations of history. In struggling we come closer to God

---

5. See question 2E.
6. Acts 3:1–10.

and are blessed.[7] We die to ourselves. The Church dies to herself. And we are raised to new life in Christ. To follow Jesus means to go through suffering and death, not to skirt them.

St. Augustine put the Christian position best: "In essentials unity, in the rest diversity, in all things charity." In discerning the essentials, in learning to accept diversity, and in preserving unity we come to wholeness as we give ear to the Spirit of God, the gift of Jesus and the Father to us.

3B. Why do we need a Church?

It is a commonly held opinion that the Church is an unnecessary hindrance between the individual and God. Why should we need any mediation between God and ourselves other than Jesus Christ? This idea is a corruption of the Reformation critique.

Sometimes Martin Luther and the other reformers are pictured standing against the Catholic Church in favor of the individual. Yet every one of the Protestant Reformers set up a Church, and within a generation the Lutheran and Calvinist Churches were as doctrinal and authoritarian as the Catholic.

Catholicism does not see the Church standing between the individual and God. When many people think of the Church they think only of the buildings, the rituals, the ministers and bureaucracy of the Church. But the Church is truly the pilgrim people of God.[8] The Church is the entire Christian community spread throughout the world today and reaching back to encompass all past generations.

How else can we come to know the good news except through the Church? If we read the Bible we are reading a book written

---

7. Gn 32:23–32.
8. De Ecclesia 2.

by Church members and declared Scripture by the Church. If we hear the good news from another, chances are that person is a Christian and so a member of the Church.

God most fully reveals himself through a human person—Jesus Christ. God spoke fully our language. Is it not then reasonable that we should today come to know God through other human beings—the followers of Jesus who gather together in his name? There is no way to avoid the Church and enter into relationship with the Christian God.

Paul uses the body of Christ as an image of the Church.[9] Some are hands, some are the mind, some are the heart. And just as it would be ridiculous for the mind to see itself independent of the rest of the body, so would it be for Christians to see themselves in isolation from the Church.

Some claim that the Church is not a visible institution but rather an invisible community of all true Christians. Yet the New Testament Church is quite visible. Paul's letters reveal it as sinful in its various members. The New Testament Church appears no purer or more sinless than the later institution.

If God was so concerned about purity, why did he dirty himself by becoming flesh and blood? As St. Ambrose marveled in the *Te Deum,* God did not shrink from the virgin's womb. Jesus wasn't afraid to entrust his vision to the likes of Peter who seemed never to understand quite what he was getting at. He even put Peter at the head of the community. God says to us in Jesus that he loves us and trusts us in spite of our sinfulness. Indeed he has accepted that sinfulness and refuses to let it come between him and us.

The Church is human, sinful, finite, spiteful, wrong-headed at times; it is a stumbling block to our belief. But was it so easy to

---

9. 1Cor 12:12–36.

see the Godhead in the flesh and blood Jesus? Many met him
and did not believe that he was anything out of the ordinary.
Yet Christians recognize that in this limited human being God
came among us. What prevents us from believing that God is
still among us through this limited Christian community,
indeed that God works and manifests himself in his Spirit,
giving breath and glory through limited beings like you and
me?

Behind opposition to the Church lurks a belief that humanity is
first and foremost individual. The West has developed and
exalted the individual more than any other culture. And the
individual person is indeed sacred. But there is a cost as well, in
alienation and the loss of tradition and community which
ground the individual in society.

The Hebrew Scriptures show a God who reveals himself to a
people. Indeed God creates this people Israel. The nation is
constantly addressed. The individual is always considered a part
of the whole, not a whole unto himself or herself.

Similarly Jesus in his ministry builds a community around him.
He doesn't deal with individuals in isolation. Indeed he calls
individuals into this new community.

Humans are social animals: individuals in community. Take
away the community, and the individual suffers. Many
problems in America today stem from lack of rather than too
much community. People feel isolated, adrift, estranged from
each other; goals are ephemeral and unsatisfying.

Catholics find the Spirit of Jesus today primarily among his
followers. The followers can come between the person and
God. Churches indulge in the same sinful actions as the rest of
society. But where else can we experience a God who teaches us
the supreme value of compassion, love, forgiveness, and
breaking bread in thanksgiving?

Churches can and have interfered and usurped power not theirs. But these situations are corrected by the Holy Spirit. Witness how often the Church has thrown off corruption and been renewed. That the Church becomes corrupt is no reason to throw her out altogether. We cannot see the human face of God shown us by Jesus except through the other human beings who have encountered him.

The history of Israel portrays God's growing involvement in the human condition. He appears first in the great event of her history—bringing her from the slavery of Egypt into her own land. In the prophets God suffers with the poor and begs Israel to change her heart. Jesus is God become human, sharing our condition in its fullness. Does it make sense that suddenly God would reverse himself and be available only as Spirit, only through a book?

3C. Is the Church the kingdom of God?

Composed as it is of sinful people, the Church shares in that sinfulness. And just as human beings have a tendency to pride, to thinking we are God, so the Church takes on that pride and comes to see herself not simply as the Church but as the Kingdom itself. But although the Church and the Kingdom are related they are not the same thing.

This tendency was notable in the Catholic Church when she acquired great power, both spiritual and secular. Christendom and the Holy Roman Empire were founded upon the assumption that the Church and the Kingdom are the same.

But the tendency is hardly limited to established Churches. It exists in fundamentalist groups unwilling to accept the notion of a visible Church because of all the unreformed people among the membership. For them the true Church is composed of the true believers, and this Church of the redeemed is the Kingdom in this world.

Unreformed Christians in her midst have always afflicted
Christianity. Paul had to deal with such a problem.[10] As long as
these people are within the Church there is a better chance that
they might awaken to the Gospel and be converted than if they
were excluded. Thus the established Churches to this day do
not have severe demands for membership and in consequence
include the half-committed or even unconverted.

The Church is the earthly body of Christ, commissioned to
carry on his ministry of announcing the coming Kingdom. She
herself is not the Kingdom, but only its seed in our world. Her
task is to work with God for the coming of the Kingdom in
glory. Many in the Kingdom were never Christians. And there
may be Christians absent from the Kingdom.

We are sinful human beings in spite of being Christian, saved
by the mercy and love of God. And we are given a mission by
God to proclaim the good news of God's love. But entrance into
the Kingdom is not restricted to Christians. It depends upon
how we act.[11] If we act toward our brothers and sisters with
love, we are part of the Kingdom. But if we profess faith with
our mouths but do not act in love we are far from the
Kingdom. And although the Church is quite visible, the
Kingdom is hidden in our midst as yeast in bread.[12]

3D. Aren't all Christians priests?

The reformers contended that all Christians are priests of Jesus
Christ. On the other hand there is only one priest—Jesus Christ
himself. Whatever the argument, the point was against the
ordained ministry. When pressured the Church responded by
defending the ordained ministry and downplaying the
priesthood of all believers exalted by the reformers. But in spite

---

10. 1 Cor 5:1–13.
11. Mt 25:31–46.
12. Mt 13:33.

of theology, the Reformation Churches developed an ordained ministry and bureaucracy, for such structures are vital to a community's functioning.

The Second Vatican Council was able to reconsider and, with the heat of controversy past, come to a more balanced position. The Reformation Churches are also able to admit the necessity for an ordained ministry. Thus today agreement is growing over this Reformation issue as well as others.

The primary priest (and indeed the only true priest) for Christians is Jesus Christ. The priest acts as a mediator between God and the people. He offers prayers and performs rituals which express the people's needs and which mediate God's response through blessings, healing, and forgiveness. Jesus fulfills this priestly role perfectly through his life and ministry. Indeed Christians see Jesus' death as a free sacrifice of his life to restore a lost unity with God.

Although Jesus is no longer physically present on earth his ministry continues. The good news is proclaimed; the sick are healed; captives are set free; sinners are forgiven. Jesus passed this ministry on to his original disciples who in turn have passed it on to those who followed. This ministry is not restricted to the official ministers. It is rather a ministry given to each Christian in baptism.

We are baptized not only for ourselves. Each sacrament exists not simply for the person who receives it but for the whole world. We do not need to focus upon ourselves. Our needs are known to our Father and are addressed by him. Thus we can turn our attention to those still in need.

In becoming Christians we respond to Jesus' call to join his ministry. We have experienced something of the Kingdom through Jesus and the Church. Now we are in turn commissioned to carry that good news into our world. Christians share in the one priesthood of Jesus Christ. As he proclaimed the good news through his stories and miracles, so we are called to proclaim the good news through our lives. As he forgave, so we in turn forgive. As he healed, so we in turn heal. As he loved, so we in turn love. We are not different priests than Jesus; we share in his priesthood.

How do we undertake our ministry of proclaiming the good news? Are we to go from door to door evangelizing? We certainly accept the commission by Jesus to proclaim the Gospel to all people so that all may hear the good news. But such a proclamation is not the gift of every Christian. It requires work, study and training to become an effective missionary. Thus Christian communities set up programs to train people for this ministry. Thus have arisen professional ministries within the Churches.

The priesthood of all believers is not necessarily called to evangelize in this particular way. Every Christian is called first of all to proclaim the good news through life style. It is more important to witness to the Kingdom by living Kingdom values in our daily life than to preach such a Kingdom.

The greatest evangelization is a life lived in love and joy. Such a life attracts others to ask what enables us to live this way. And when asked we can share the message of Jesus that motivates us. All too often Christians speak the Gospel rather than live it. Of course it is easier. But we are called to live in the Kingdom, not necessarily to preach it.

Jesus did not limit his own ministry to preaching. Indeed preaching occupies a relatively minor aspect. He tells stories of the Kingdom—he is a poet. He forgives sins—he is a reconciler. He heals the sick, physically, spiritually, mentally—he is a healer. He is a teacher. He sides with the poor and oppressed— he is in a way a social worker. He feeds the hungry—he is a nurturer. All form part of his priesthood. And each of us has gifts enabling us to join in one or more of these ministries.

Too often Christians have made ministry religious. But Jesus is not a religious person. He reserves his most severe words for the religious leaders of his day. His message addresses common people in their common life. And we common people are enabled by him to continue his ministry today.

3E. Why do we need ordained priests and bishops?

As Jesus went from place to place he spoke to the crowds of people proclaiming in word and sign the Kingdom breaking into our world through him. From these people he called some to forsake their former way of life and follow him. Not limited to the twelve disciples, these included women. They remained with Jesus, learning from him, growing close. Jesus sent these people out into the countryside to proclaim the good news and to cast out demons in his name.[13] Within this group were twelve forming a cadre—the disciples. And within these a special place falls to Peter, James and John—an inner circle. Of these Jesus appoints Peter the leader.

Jesus sees his own mission in terms of Israel's tradition. Indeed his choosing of twelve disciples emphasizes the new Israel which God is creating in him. Israel the patriarch had twelve sons, and they became the leaders of the twelve tribes.

Jesus in accord with his time considers people in relation to society. An individual in isolation is not even considered. That possibility has only arisen in our modern world—and with it many modern miseries.

After Easter he commissions his disciples to carry the good news to the rest of humanity. The disciples go out. And as people hear this good news and become Christians they form new communities.

------

13. Lk 9:1–6; 10:1–16.

Every community has a structure. There are roles with people selected to do the necessary tasks. It was no different in the Christian communities. Who would guide the community and pass on the faith to newcomers? Who would preside at meetings? Who would lead in prayer? Who would break bread for the community as Jesus had requested? Who would keep discipline?

So offices and official ministries arose. Their growth is seen in the different strata of the New Testament. The picture of the Church in the early Corinthian letters is different from a later letter such as Timothy. In later New Testament writings a Church structure emerges with bishops, deacons and presbyters.[14]

That structure continued to develop after the New Testament period. For why should it suddenly be arrested at a certain time? And at what time? With the ministry of Jesus? Then the developments of the letters to Timothy are corruptions. With the end of the New Testament? But on what authority, since only a much later Church would define the New Testament canon?[15]

God works through these natural structures of human society. He used Israel's institutions including monarchy and priesthood. These structures were sometimes sinful and in need of reformation. But Israel's institutions were not regarded simply as necessary evils. She took pride in her kings, priests, and scribes.

The constant thrust of Scripture shows God working through his creation, through the human order. He becomes human in Jesus—uses human words and emotions to reach us. Why should he stop now? Indeed the evidence of the New

---

14. 1 Tm 3:1–16.
15. See question 1J.

Testament is that he didn't. Jesus passed on his ministry to his disciples.[16] They in turn passed it on to individuals within the different Churches.[17] And that ordained ministry has continued to serve the Christian communities to this day.

At times these official ministries become embedded in human sinfulness. Bad priests betray and pervert their office. Proud men forget that Jesus defined leadership in terms of service rather than power.[18] The official ministry has often exalted itself at the expense of the priesthood of all Christians. But such perversions are corrected as God raises prophets in his Church to return her to the Gospel.

All Christians share in the priesthood of Jesus Christ with their lives and various talents.[19] The ordained ministries serve the people of God in various specialized ways: as teachers, priests, missionaries, healers. They do not supplant the larger ministry but support it.

3F. Is there salvation outside the Church?

It has sometimes been maintained that Catholics believe that only Catholics are saved. But such is not the case. Indeed earlier this century in Boston Fr. Feeney was silenced for preaching just such an idea. In fact the Catholic understanding of salvation is much broader than that of other Christians.

Fundamentalists are quite clear. To be saved the person must come to acknowledge Jesus as one's personal Lord and Savior. But what about all those people who through no fault of their own will never have a chance to hear the good news? They will

---

16. Jn 20:21–23.
17. Acts 1:15–16; 6:1–7.
18. Jn 13:1–20.
19. See question 3D.

not be saved. Thus the tremendous thrust behind missionary activity.

While catholicism certainly believes that one is a Christian because one believes in Jesus as Lord and Savior, it sees this as but the first step in becoming a member of Jesus' community. The God of Israel is God of a people, not merely a private God of individuals. Jesus forms a community of followers. By becoming Christians we are joined to the body of Christ on this earth. This body is the Church.[20]

Catholics view the body of Christ on earth as those communities which acknowledge the Pope as the successor of St. Peter whom Jesus appointed as head and leader of the apostles.[21] Thus the visible body of Christ is that Church in communion with the Pope.

But what about the other Christian Churches? Are they part of the body of Christ in some way? To answer this question the Church views herself as a series of concentric circles, one within another. In the inner circle stands the Pope—a sign of unity going back to Jesus. Around him is found the Roman Catholic Church and those Eastern Churches (called Uniate) in communion with Rome. Next come the Orthodox Churches who hold the same faith but who are in schism. Next come the various Protestant Churches who cling to the traditional definition of faith in the Nicene Creed. Together these Churches form official Christendom.

But the Church does not stop here. There are sects who, while they do not profess the traditional Creed, still seek to follow Jesus. These are groups like the Mormons and the Jehovah's Witnesses. These are part of the Church.

---

20. See question 3B.
21. See question 1G.

Nor does the Church stop here. What about the Jews?[22] First to be called by God, they stand in a special relation to God. From our perspective we acknowledge that somehow the Jews are also a part of the Church. And Islam also shares a special part of the covenant since they too trace their lineage from Abraham. How are these groups part of the Church? That we cannot say. But somehow they too are a part of God's people because they too trace their origin to the same covenant.

Furthermore, there were covenants before Abraham. The covenant with Noah was made with all people.[23] And are we to say that God does not love people who are not part of these later covenants? Jesus, following Isaiah[24] and Jonah,[25] corrects Israel's understanding of herself to show that God does not restrict himself to Israel.[26] He has chosen Israel not for anything she is in herself,[27] but to be a sign to the other nations of his love.[28]

All too often Israel considered her election as something that set her apart, making her special. She exalted herself at the expense of the others. Christians have done the same. But this betrays God's choice of us. We are chosen to be a sign to others. We are not chosen because God rejects his other people.

So what of the other great world faiths? Only in the last century have Christians actually encountered these faiths.[29] And we find much beauty in them. Catholics believe that these faiths too are good and in some way, like Israel, a preparation for the full truth of Jesus. So they too are part of the Church. Thus as

---

22. Declaration on Non-Christian Religions.
23. Gn 9:8–17.
24. Is 25:6–12.
25. Jon 4:1–11.
26. Mt 8:5–13.
27. Dt 7:7–9.
28. Is 49:6.
29. See question 5J.

catholics define the Church there is no salvation outside, but in some mysterious way the Church encompasses all humanity.

But do these people have to come to believe in Jesus in order to be saved? While we believe that no one is saved except through Jesus Christ, we do not believe that a person needs to know this consciously to be saved. Is it a person's fault that he or she is born in a land or a time with no opportunity to hear the Gospel? Does God love that person any less than he loves us? Jesus tells us that such is not the case. The God who goes out in search of the lost sheep is not one who binds himself by hard and fast rules.[30]

It is God's will that all people should be saved.[31] With such an understanding we must look to see how God is accomplishing his will. Our missionary activity will not achieve God's will for universal salvation, for it is unlikely that at any time all people will become Christians. And millions have already died without the Gospel. So we must look to see other ways in which God is accomplishing his plan.

To understand how these people are saved, Catholicism in the past spoke of various ways of baptism. Christians are saved by being incorporated into the body of Christ through baptism by water. But there were cases in the early days of Christianity when people came to believe in Jesus but were martyred before they could receive baptism. Were these people lost? No, said the Church. And she spoke of them as having undergone a baptism of fire: martyrdom.

But what of people who never heard the Gospel, or heard it in such a way they could not accept its truth? If these people sincerely tried to live doing good and avoiding evil, they too were saved. They were saved by Jesus Christ though they did

---

30. Lk 15:4–7.
31. Nostra Aetate 1 and 2.

not know him. And she spoke of this as baptism of desire. If they had understood the Gospel they would have embraced it.

The Catholic Church acknowledges that no one is saved except through Jesus Christ. We are saved as part of the human society, not merely as individuals, so the Church in her fullness, including all humanity, is the vehicle of salvation. But she does not put limits upon the love of God. And going by what she has learned of God's love from Jesus she can imagine God saving his entire beloved creation.

Which vision seems more in accord with Jesus—one in which God's love is without boundaries, or one in which strict requirements must be met which in reality only a minority throughout history or in the world today can satisfy?

3G. Why do Catholics have devotion to Mary and the saints?

Catholics think of the Church as the body of Christ which joins all together. We are saved as a people, joined as brothers and sisters in Jesus Christ. This community extends both in space and in time. We are joined with all Christians throughout the world today in the same community, especially with all Roman Catholics in a visible unity with the Pope. But we are united as well with all Christians who have ever lived. Our God is a God of the living, not of the dead. Those who have gone before us are still a part of the Church.

As members of a family we support and help one another. We keep one another in mind in our prayers. You pray for your friends who are sick. And if you are going through difficulties, it is comforting to ask a fellow Christian to keep you in his or her prayers.

From this natural action it is a short step to the catholic practice of asking the saints to pray for us. They are in the presence of God. So we ask them to keep us in mind in their own prayers. It is as simple as that. We need not limit those praying for us to the canonized saints of the Church. Relatives who have gone before us into God's presence are still in the Church and can remember us, just as we remember them. The sharing of prayers is an expression of community, and that community is hardly limited to the present.

The saints function in other ways. They are examples of Christian living, providing concrete enfleshments of Jesus and his Kingdom in various times and places. Thus the saints inspire us in the creation of our own Christian living.

Through St. Francis of Assisi we see facets of the Christian faith beautifully illumined. Jesus taught that money often inhibits following him and belonging to the Kingdom.[32] Once a rich young man sought to follow Jesus totally, but when Jesus told him to divest himself of his wealth he was unable to do so and went away.[33] Francis was a rich young man who did follow this command. He devoted himself to Lady Poverty, showing how truly rich a Christian life might be without wealth. He also made Jesus more human and lovable, for Francis first set up a manger scene at Christmas. Through his followers he created a Renaissance in both Church and culture.

No one prays to the saints. Prayer is only addressed to God. But we can ask the saints to pray for us. However there is no necessity to do this. It is simply something which Catholics have room for.

Mary has generated great devotion through the Catholic and broader Christian world. She was chosen to be the mother of the Lord. The New Testament writers see her as the embodiment of Israel herself. It is natural that she should have attracted devotion. Again catholics do not pray to her. They

---

32. Lk 16:13.
33. Mk 10:17–22.

honor her and ask her to pray for them. This can be seen in the most popular Marian devotion—the Hail Mary—which concludes with the words: "Pray for us sinners now and at the hour of our death." It is not necessary to have devotion to Mary, but every Christian must hold her in the highest regard, for she bore the Son of God.

3H. Why do Christians go to Church?

We have seen that a person comes to know Jesus and Christianity through the Christian community. Certainly the crux is the person's conversion to Jesus Christ. But conversion can only occur in the context of the Christian community. Church gives birth to conversion. So initially a person goes to church in order to learn about Jesus.

Jesus is present in the Christian community.[34] We come together in community first of all to remember Jesus and his great work. We gather on Sunday in commemoration of that first Easter Sunday. We gather on other days to acknowledge and remember other great events of our salvation or our tradition.

One of Jesus' key teachings is the attitude of thanksgiving. Jesus was always giving thanks to God. And this attitude leads toward real happiness. Thus Christian worship is primarily a giving thanks to God for all his blessings. Indeed the word "Eucharist" means "thanksgiving" in Greek. And among catholics the Eucharist forms the center of Christian worship and praise.

One of Jesus' ministries was reconciliation and forgiveness. We hurt and fail one another. We may believe the good news of the Kingdom, but we are still sinful. So we come together as a community to be forgiven and reconciled by Christ. As

---

34. Mt 18:20.

Christians we are eager to admit our sinfulness, for we know it leads not to condemnation but forgiveness. In our community we experience that forgiveness.

Jesus was a great healer. And all of us at some time or other are in need of healing. As Christians we pray for healing. And the presence of Jesus among us carries on his ministry.

In short Christians gather in Church to share in the presence of Jesus Christ. We do not worship some disembodied God long gone from the earth. Our God continues to be among his people leading them in thanksgiving, forgiving them, nourishing them, healing them, sending them forth to share the good news with his other creatures.

3I. What about sinful Christians and even sinful Churches?

Christians have heard the good news and committed their lives to Jesus. They are neither perfect nor sinless. And in any given community some are deeply committed to the Gospel while the commitment of others seems less than wholehearted.

The issue crops up throughout Christian history.[35] A fully converted Church would be wonderful. But human beings are not so simple. Who is to judge whether a conversion is authentic or not? Only God.[36]

Throughout history groups filled with committed Christians have split off from the larger Churches. Yet within a generation these resemble the established Churches. The Methodist Church—today regarded as establishment—began as a group of enthusiasts. What will happen to some of the cults of today? The Unification Church of Reverend Moon—today a cult—

---

35. For example, the Montanists.
36. Rom 14:10–12.

might within a few generations be as mainstream lukewarm as the Methodists, Episcopalians or Roman Catholics. Sinful human nature is the irreducible constant.

So the Catholic and other Churches have a fairly open policy of membership. They would prefer fully committed Christians. These Churches frequently call to renewal and conversion. Lent is the prime example. The Second Vatican Council shows an entire Church undergoing renewal. These Churches tolerate sinners because they know that God loves and seeks out these sinners so that they may be converted.

No group, no matter how pure, how converted, is without sin. And it is a dangerous sign when any group proclaims its righteousness. Who are we to know what lies in the hearts of other persons? On the surface they may seem quite unconverted. But do we know what they are struggling with, what they have been through, how they respond? Only God does. When any group holds itself up as the only bastion of purity or real Christianity, chances are that that group has fallen into the worst sin of all: pride—to put oneself or one's church in the place of God.

3J. Why remain in a Church that is sinful and even irrelevant?

Churches are composed of sinners who have heard and accepted in whatever way they are able the word of God. These communities are sinful: they have promoted prejudice, they have betrayed Gospel values. Sometimes they are simply irrelevant. Many have observed that people outside the Christian community act more like Christ than those who bear his name. Why stay and affiliate with such a Church?

But who is the Church? Often Christians see it as an organization or institution to which they belong. The Church is primarily the clergy: the officials. Yet these truly are not the

Church. The Church is not a them, it is us. And just as we are
in need of conversion, so is the Church. But where will this
recommitment to the Gospel come from? Usually it comes not
from the officials but the grassroots—from the saints.

Looking at the Church as us rather than them, we take power
over our own life and faith. Yes, officials can deaden a
Christian community. But even they are open to conversion.
And Christianity does not depend upon her officials for the
faith no matter how important they see themselves. Community
is people. Community is us. And within any Christian group
unless it is totally dead, the Gospel is giving life.

A Christian may be at times without a sustaining community.
Such situations happen and must be suffered through with the
help of God. But just as people are not meant to be alone and
isolated, so are Christians meant to be in community. Alone
who will comfort us, encourage us, challenge us, nourish us?
These come best from other people, not from a book no matter
how holy.

And throughout history even in the darkest ages the faith has
not been lost. In those times God raises up saints to shine once
more the purity of the Gospel and to bring the Church back to
her source. If we find ourselves in a sinful or irrelevant
community, for our own health we may have to go into exile.
But our real mission is to that community. Our mission: to
nourish there the seeds of the Gospel. To leave is to give up.

Furthermore the Church is more than the local community. A
Catholic is part of a larger community than the local
congregation. And in the Roman Catholic Church as a whole
today the witness to the Gospel is something to be proud of.
The Church of Poland daily struggles against government
oppression in the cause of individual rights and liberties. The
emerging liberation movements of Latin America inspired by a
renewed Church are attentive to the cry of the poor. In our
own country the Catholic Church joins in the increased concern

over the arms race and is identifying with the oppressed and disadvantaged in our economic system.

The struggle for God's justice is hardly won. Issues within the Church need addressing—the rights of women for one. But justice never comes easily. As Christians we align ourselves with God, dedicating ourselves to the making of justice. In solidarity we make progress. Isolated we have no hope. God calls us to prepare the way for his Kingdom. Our mission is to build and nurture community. Far from irrelevant, the Church's mission today may spell the difference between continued life and nuclear holocaust.

Christian Life

4A. What is a sacrament?

Sacraments lie at the heart of catholic experience. For the major catholic doctrine is the incarnation—that in Jesus God took on full humanity. Since in Jesus God took this step he continues to encounter us on our own ground. The man Jesus is not on earth today, but we meet him in certain holy moments called sacraments.

The catholic looking at creation sees in spite of sin the marks of the Creator. A catholic experiences God in a beautiful sunset, in a pagan philosopher like Plato, in the various religions of the world, in sexuality. These are not the full revelation of God discovered only in Jesus, but they are intimations pointing toward their Creator. They sing his praise.

And certain events are charged with the holy: birth, coming to adulthood, marriage, forgiveness, healing, service, even the celebration of a family meal. How much of Jesus' ministry was spent enjoying and celebrating such moments! He was criticized as being too much of a party person, eating with the wrong people at that.[1] He enjoins his followers to baptize in his name,[2] and to remember him whenever they share meals together.[3] These have become the sacraments of baptism and Eucharist.

---

1. Lk 7:33–35.
2. Mt 28:19.
3. Lk 22:19–20.

As the early Church meditated upon Jesus and passed on his experience, she recognized the Lord's presence in other holy moments. In the forgiveness of sins and the healing of the sick she continued Jesus' major ministries. In service to the community and in the love of husband and wife she came to see the Lord's transforming presence.

Through these sacramental moments the Christian today encounters and is transformed by Jesus Christ. God is not limited to these moments—he is free to encounter us where he will. But the Church pledges that God is always present in these sacramental events. When we are baptized Christ is truly present, receiving us into his community. When we share Eucharist Christ is each time truly present. Whether we are present to receive him is another matter.

4B. What is baptism?

Baptism initiates a person into the Christian community. All Christians believe in the necessity of baptism since Jesus mandates it in the Gospels.[4]

Conversion is a process. A person needs to be adequately prepared: to hear the Gospel, to experience the Christian community, to learn Christian methods of prayer and spirituality, and to experience how the Gospel changes our life. This process takes place in the catechumenate.

Christian initiation is celebrated at the Easter vigil and includes the sacraments of baptism, confirmation and Eucharist. In being baptized the person is immersed in a pool of water, symbolizing being joined to Jesus in his death and raised with him to new life in the resurrection. While some Churches for practicality practice baptism by pouring water over the

---

4. Mt. 28:19.

forehead, the full meaning of the rite is only seen in immersion, and the Roman Church recognizes immersion as the norm.[5] The person then is anointed and celebrates the Eucharist with the community.

Furthermore Catholics believe that baptism effects what it signifies. A sacrament is an encounter with the living Christ. Some Christians believe that baptism is only a sign and that nothing actually happens in the action other than the person's testimony that he or she has given his or her life to Jesus. For the catholic it certainly means this, but it also claims the person as Christ's and a full member in the Church. It forgives sins and offers a new beginning.

The established Churches also practice infant baptism. While the fullness of baptism is only found in adults, the Churches baptize infants so they may be raised within the Church. They are baptized not on their own faith but on the faith of their parents and godparents. Then, raised within the Christian community, they appropriate the faith for themselves.

As infant baptism became more the rule, confirmation was separated from baptism in the Western Church and considered a separate sacrament. It is really the completion of baptism, but was separated so that as baptized children grew up they would be able to affirm their baptism and realize its fullness in conferring this sacrament. It imparts the gift of the Holy Spirit and commissions the person to be a full Christian—one who lives for others and accepts his or her mission from Christ to carry the good news through his or her life and example.

4C. Is Christ truly present in the Eucharist?

For catholics Jesus is truly present in the Eucharist. Conflict arose when Christians attempted to explain just how Jesus was

---

5. Rite of Christian Initiation of Adults.

present. But going back to the words of institution in the Gospels[6] and in Paul[7] we believe that in the Eucharist the bread and wine become Jesus Christ. We call this belief the real presence. Whereas in the past attention was concentrated upon the bread and wine, today the Church emphasizes a much richer awareness of Christ's presence.[8]

Christ is present in the Eucharist and other celebrations in the Gospel. For this reason and to witness our belief in the resurrection, we stand when the gospel is proclaimed. The living Lord is present in this proclamation. He speaks to our condition today and leads us just as the earthly Jesus taught and led his disciples.

In the Eucharist Jesus is further present in the person of the priest.[9] Imitating Jesus at the Last Supper, the priest is an image of Christ. Of course he is not Christ himself. He is sinful and selfish. But in the performance of this ritual his actual life is irrelevant. He is taken up into a role larger than himself.

Christ uses the priest to feed his people. When the priest or deacon proclaims the Gospel it is not his words but the word of God that is proclaimed. When the priest forgives, it is not by his own power but that of Christ speaking through him. When at the end of the Eucharist we are sent forth to continue the work of Jesus, the priest does not send us forth—he is the mouthpiece of Jesus commissioning us this day to be about his work. That the priest is unworthy does not prevent Christ from ministering through him. We are all unworthy receptacles for God's grace, yet God does not shrink from using us.

And Christ is present in the bread and the wine—the elements of the Eucharist. This is simply following the words of

---

6. Mk 14:22–25; Mt 26:26–29; Lk 22:19–20; Jn 6:51–58.
7. 1 Cor 11:23–25.
8. See also question 2J.
9. See question 3E.

institution in the Gospels and Paul—words Paul had in turn received from those in the Church before him.[10] Catholics believe that Jesus is present in the bread and wine through transubstantiation. This means at its simplest that while the elements still seem to be bread and wine, in reality they are the body of Christ. The key question is whether Jesus Christ is truly present in this action.

4D. What is a sin?

Certain Christians talk a lot about sin. Just what is sin and what constitutes a sin? There are various kinds of sin. We have already discussed the condition of original sin.[11]

Because we live in the state and environment of original sin, all of us eventually commit sins against one another. For a catholic sin is always social—it is an action committed against another person or group. There is no such thing as a sin committed solely against God. Things are sinful not because they make God angry but because they hurt our brothers and sisters and ourselves. Here is our primary definition of sin.

When God brought the slaves out of Egypt he promised to make them a people, and to found this new people he gave them a charter in the law. Part of the law concerns a moral code. Its essence is the Ten Commandments which Christians believe provide the foundation for moral living.

However as Paul points out the Commandments do not create sins.[12] They simply reveal what is sinful. Prior to the law a person might claim to act in ignorance. In the light of the Commandments however the action is known as sin. The Ten

---

10. 1 Cor 11:23.
11. See question 2A.
12. Rom 7:7.

Commandments form a basis for society whether it be ancient Israel or the Church.

In addition the golden rule of Jesus shapes our lives and behavior. Do unto others as you would have them do unto you.[13] And Jesus further says that the entire law can be reduced to two commandments: Love God and love your neighbor as yourself.[14] Love is the supreme motivation in Christian morality. Christianity doesn't settle for a minimum morality: do this and you've done your duty. The Christian tries to act out of love. And of course love knows no bounds.

Catholics go on to distinguish two kinds of sin. One is mortal sin, which cuts the person off from human society and from God. To commit a mortal sin the person first must be aware of its seriousness and sinfulness. Second, the person must be free to choose to do this action. It cannot be compelled by circumstances. Third, the action must be objectively serious.

Believing that stepping on cracks in the pavement is mortally sinful does not make it so. Accidentally running over a pedestrian is not a mortal sin. Of course the driver may be sinning mortally if driving while drunk. And even if the action is not a mortal sin the person may have severe guilt which needs healing. But for a mortal sin, all three conditions must be fulfilled.

Now most people do not commit mortal sins as a matter of course. But simply because we are not mortally sinful does not mean that we are good. Thousands of lesser sins committed daily bind us in our selfishness and misery. And although called venial these sins are not without consequence. For one thing they keep us from experiencing the Kingdom of God.

---

13. Lk 6:31.
14. Mt 23:34–40.

4E. Why should anyone have to confess to a priest?

Catholics believe that a person in mortal sin[15] needs to go to confession to a priest and receive absolution. Only in the sacrament is there full assurance of forgiveness.

But what is sin actually? It is an action which alienates a person from the human community. When we have sinned we have broken the social contract. We have lied, stolen, or hurt a fellow human being. We need reconciliation not only with the injured, but with society itself. Christians belong to the society of the Church. Sin alienates us from the community of Jesus. And since that community is visible we need some means of re-establishing our relationship in the community. The priest acting for the community reconciles us to the community and to God.

God is not tied to the priest in order to forgive our sins. He can and does forgive us outside the sacrament of reconciliation. The sacrament offers concrete assurance of God's forgiveness. As embodied creatures we experience through our bodies. Concrete bodily signs communicate what is happening to us. In confession we actually speak our sins, hearing in return words of reconciliation. We are touched as well in a physical expression of God's forgiveness.

Confession is a beautiful experience of God's love for us. To admit we have sinned, to acknowledge our selfishness is difficult. We would rather not look at these parts of ourselves. And most people left on their own do not look too closely at their concrete sins. It is easy to admit that I am a sinner. It is more difficult to articulate just where I have sinned. Yet would we go to a doctor, simply say we are sick and expect him to heal us? Without the specifics of our illness treatment is impossible.

---

15. See question 4D.

And before we can move out of our own sins we need to confront them and bring them to God.

But the difficulty is small compared with the consolations of confession. Isn't it more comforting to hear forgiveness from the human voice than to rely upon what we think God might be doing for us? He spoke forgiveness through the words and actions of Jesus to the people of that day. Why should not the same words and actions be available to Christians of our day? They are in the community of Jesus.

Jesus promised the disciples the power to forgive sins, but it was a long process before the sacrament of reconciliation emerged. At first forgiveness of sins was tied strictly to baptism which forgives all a person's sins.

Then in the third and fourth century the concept of readmitting sinful Christians developed. Sinners were excommunicated from the Christian community to bring them to their senses. If they then showed repentance, they were given a public penance lasting a year or more. Once that penance was completed, sinners were received back into the Church by the bishop on Holy Thursday.

Later in the Middle Ages another practice arose in Ireland, spread by missionary monks. People would go to the holy men for counseling and direction in Christian living. In doing so they would also confess their sins. The priest imposed a penance and advised the penitent. This form became quite popular.

The Council of Trent was forced to deal with the issue of confession because the reformers had denied its sacramentality. The council declared it a sacrament and laid down rules for its proper celebration. Indeed the confessional or box which Catholics used until recently was developed to protect the penitent's anonymity.

The Second Vatican Council renewed penance, and new forms of forgiveness are coming into being today. Penance services emphasize the communal nature of sin and forgiveness. Renewal of private confession moves it out of the confessional because the darkness and closeness of the box do not adequately symbolize the joy that reconciliation brings. A renewed understanding of the Eucharist recognizes it as the normal method of reconciliation in the Christian community.

The history of confession demonstrates how creatively the Church has responded to God's gift of forgiveness. Jesus intended the forgiveness of sins to be a part of his community.[16] But how that action manifests concretely has varied according to the insight of the community and the needs of the times.

4F. How does a Christian make a decision?

What goes into a moral decision? Each person learns right from wrong as part of growing up. Our parents, schools, and society in general have certain ideas concerning right and wrong behavior. Exposed to these opinions we either accept or reject them.

Rejecting them finds us alienated from society since our views conflict. Society labels such people sociopathic. But most of us adopt pretty much the views of our parents and society. At certain points in life, particularly in late adolescence, we may rebel against accepted views. Our challenge may lead us to modify or change our own moral outlook.

Such reassessments may be small or significant in nature. During the 1960's many young people claimed to reject the value systems, including the morality of their elders,

---

16. Mt 16:19.

particularly in regard to sexuality and the value of peace. Some of these changes came to be reflected in the culture at large. Today society's understanding of sexuality is not quite what it was in the 1950's.

A moral code is not unchanging, handed on from on high. Being intimately connected with people it changes and adjusts to the contemporary situation. Acceptable behavior at one time (slavery, for example) becomes a heinous offense to a later morality. Today we see challenges to traditional notions of sexuality, war and peace, racial and sexual discrimination. These challenges often produce anxiety and confusion. There are no clear-cut answers. Society has not yet developed a new moral outlook, so there is ambiguity: some people clinging to the traditional code, others experimenting with different options.

How does a Christian fit into this pattern? Like everyone else we acquire morality from our environment as we mature. Growing up within a Christian household and community our morals will reflect those of the community. There will be an additional Christian component along with the other moral influences. And the contents will be flavored by the particular community. For a Baptist card playing and drinking will be regarded as wrong while being quite acceptable to a Catholic.

Some Christians claim that the Bible gives clear moral teaching. Therefore they say that there can be such a thing as an objective Christian morality supposedly valid for all time. But is this so? Take just the instance of slavery. St. Paul is comfortable with the idea. He tells those who are slaves in his communities to become good slaves and to serve their masters well.[17]

Yet would any Christian today in good conscience support slavery? What has happened? The morality of slavery has

---

17. 1 Cor 7:20–24.

evolved from the time of St. Paul. We have come to see the intrinsic value of freedom for every individual human being. No longer can we countenance the exploitation of some human beings for the benefit of others.

Today a new moral vision, looking beyond the traditional marks of slavery, perceives the oppression of third world peoples by the second and first world. Perhaps tomorrow the kinds of economic exploitation acceptable today will be as immoral as slavery.

The Bible cannot hope to address all these situations. What it says to the world of its time does not necessarily apply to our much different world. So at least for catholics the Bible is not a simple code of morality speaking to each situation.

A catholic receives aid in making a moral decision from Scripture and the Church's moral teaching. Throughout history the Church has been forced to decide moral issues, and that teaching contains a great wisdom. And so the catholic would look to the Christian community—to individual members such as clergy and counselors and to friends for help in reaching a moral decision. Finally the catholic must listen to the voice of his or her own conscience.[18]

4G. What happens when conscience conflicts with Church teaching?

Catholics have a reputation for being forced to do what the Church says no matter what. But while certain catholics may feel this way it has never been official teaching. A catholic is obliged to follow his or her conscience in a moral teaching even if Church teaching is contrary to conscience.

---

18. See question 4G.

The human conscience is as close as we come to hearing the Holy Spirit within us. Therefore we should not violate the voice of conscience even though it may be malformed. To do so is to risk going against the Spirit of God.

Our conscience is formed in the maturing process. It is shaped by environment, our parents primarily, then institutions such as schools and churches. These different groups teach us their understanding of right and wrong, and as we grow to maturity we by and large incorporate that understanding in ourselves, thus giving rise to conscience. It is hardly a simple process: people vary in what they accept and reject.

A Christian believes that the Christian tradition has evolved a high moral standard coming from the Old Testament law, the teachings of Jesus and the experience of the Christian community. Growing up in a Christian environment the person will be exposed to this vision as a part of education. If a person becomes a Christian later in life, he or she will in conversion embrace Christian values. Thus Christian teaching has great impact upon the formation of a Christian's conscience.

But conscience is not simply poured into a person. No one accepts a moral teaching completely without question. It must be compared to life experience, the person's environment, psychology, and innate moral sense. Thus it can happen that a Catholic in good conscience might adopt a moral view different from the Church as a whole.

For example, current Catholic teaching gives a nation the right to defend itself in a just war. Therefore the nation has the right to draft people into its armed forces for its protection. But a number of catholics find that they cannot support any kind of violence. They consider all war evil and cannot in good conscience serve in the armed forces. These people do not agree with the catholic moral consensus, yet the Church says that they, after careful deliberation and study of the Church's teachings, must stand with their own conscience rather than follow teachings they consider wrong. In the Vietnam War a number of bishops defended the right of catholics to seek conscientious objection.

Indeed this witness may contribute to a revision of catholic moral teaching. For the bishops themselves are wondering today if it is any longer possible to have a just war with nuclear weapons. The witnesses of today may be out of step with the official position and proved wrong. But they may also shape tomorrow's moral stance. Only time will tell. However every Christian, after careful deliberation and study of the Church's moral teaching, is obliged to form conscience as best one can and to act accordingly.

As the Protestant moralist Paul Lehmann said, the Christian should make a moral decision with the Bible in one hand, for this is the revelation of God. The other hand holds the daily newspaper—a report of the present situation with all the facts and viewpoints one can muster. And we make that decision, weighing the eternal revelation of God and our present situation on our knees in prayer.

Morality always involves risk. No one can provide us with all the right and sure answers. Morality like life itself is a mystery. And how we act flows from our spirituality.

A Catholic would add that we make our decision not on our own but in the context of the Christian community with its two thousand year moral wisdom and experience. But ultimately the decision is ours. No one can take that responsibility away from us.

4H. How does Christianity see itself in relation to the modern world?

All too often Christianity has been a world-denying faith. We were all too other-worldly. But such an attitude is not that of

Jesus. The world was created by God; thus it is good. The world and creation are not to be scorned but rather redeemed.

The rise of science put Christianity on the defensive, guarding her truths against new ideas. This is obvious in the continuing debate concerning evolution.[19]

But for the Catholic Church the tide was turned by Pope John XXIII and the Second Vatican Council. The document on the Church in the Modern World officially adopted a different attitude toward the world and her relation to it. Openness and compassion replaced suspicion and hostility. The good in modern thought is affirmed. The Gospel is seen as fulfilling the human search rather than replacing it. The various struggles for liberation are seen reflected in the liberation of the Gospel itself. The Church affirms all that echoes Gospel values, and sees herself on pilgrimage through this world as a servant aiding in the liberation and healing of the world's peoples. A new attitude even manifests itself toward the other world faiths.[20]

The Christian attitude toward the world echoes basic Christian attitudes toward nature.[21] Today we recognize goodness in groups once considered far from the Church and her message. She recognizes goodness in communist (as opposed to Soviet) thought which is concerned with the liberation of the world's peoples. She finds allies in other world faiths and shares with them. She considers science an ally rather than an enemy or rival.

In aligning she need not abandon the Gospel and her revelation. Indeed dialogue may accomplish more than argument. With communists she builds community through a

---

19. See question 5I.
20. See question 5J.
21. See question 4A.

common concern with liberation, and also questions some of the means of that liberation. With non-Christians she may share ways of prayer and meditation, and stress as well the need for active charity toward the poor. Our mission is not so much to make the world Christian as to prepare for the coming of God's Kingdom. From being colonialists we are learning to become servants—the authentic mindset of Jesus.

4I. Should a Christian be involved in social justice, politics and environmental issues?

Christianity has always been involved with social justice. The roots go back to the foundations of the Judeo-Christian tradition. A group of slaves finds liberation from Egypt and is given a land of their own.

Our tradition is largely the history of liberation in the West. The prophetic movement in Israel was concerned with social justice and the fate of the poor more than with doctrinal or religious issues. Amos asks what good are sacrifices and rituals.[22] What is needed is a change of heart concerning the oppressed.[23]

Jesus perfects Israel's experience of social justice. Of the poor himself, his ministry by and large concerns the poor who have a special place in God's affection.[24] Like the prophets before him Jesus rebuked the rich of his day for their indifference toward their poor brothers and sisters.[25] And he overcomes the social barriers. Among his followers and intimate friends are women who even today in our society are not treated equally. A Christianity without social commitment is not full Christianity.

---

22. Am 5:21–26.
23. Jer 31:31–34.
24. Lk 4:18.
25. Lk 19:45—20:4.

The history of social justice in the West is a subsidiary history of Christianity. The Church gave rise to hospitals and modern universities. Francis of Assisi touched the conscience of his age to the presence of the poor and their holiness in God's eyes. In our own day the impetus for civil rights and the black liberation movements that followed came from the Christian tradition— that same old story of the freeing of slaves.

The Catholic Church today is committed to social justice. Pope John Paul II, coming from Poland, is neither a communist nor a capitalist and criticizes both systems for putting either the state or capital before the value of the individual person. In Latin America the Church is throwing off her traditional alignment with the aristocracy to discover once more the presence of God among the poor struggling for liberation. The American bishops have prayed and studied the issue of nuclear weapons and call Christians and people of good will to ponder these important issues. Soon they will turn their attention to the American economy, and paramount will be the fate of the poor in our economic system.

Today Christian groups are often identified with the fight against abortion. But the catholic vision of the sanctity of human life encompasses much more. So catholics witness against capital punishment, against nuclear weapons, and against euthanasia. To limit one's vision of sanctity to only one issue and to actually be anti-life on other issues is not to be fully Christian.

Further, Christians must show concern for the poor deprived of life's necessities due to budget cuts and government's abandonment of welfare. While it is a matter of politics whether the government should be involved in welfare, if Christians believe that government should get out of welfare they should also aggressively take its place out of charity and their commitment to the poor.

Christianity's involvement in politics is controversial. The Catholic Church over the last hundred years lost most of her political power. And she has come to see that far from a loss it has been a gain. As the Church's political power has waned her spiritual power has grown. Loosed from the ties of politics she has been free to forthrightly proclaim the Gospel.

In our own country on the issue of nuclear weapons the bishops rely on persuasion rather than coercion. No longer do they speak expecting Catholics to obey without question. Instead they call all people to wrestle with them in hope of finding a way out of the dilemma.

Certainly politics is part of public life, and Christian values should influence the politics of Christians. But is it right for a Church or group to subvert the democratic system to push through their own ideas and values? Many means used by some Christian groups today are morally indefensible—half-truth, prejudice and vicious propaganda. Can evil ever hope to work for good? Will it not distort the good to its own ends?

We live in a time when the resources of the earth are nearing depletion and the excesses of environmental exploitation are beginning to have a significant impact upon the quality of life. Many Christians are re-examining our relationship to the earth and her resources. While traditionally Christians viewed humanity as the Lord of the earth to whom all creation is subject, today many see a deeper significance to the old story of the Garden of Eden.

Biblical scholars view the placing of the earth in humanity's care not as permission to exploit the earth but rather as a mandate to be stewards of God's creation. For too long Christians and others have seen the earth and her resources simply in terms of our own needs and pleasures. We have taken what we have needed or greedily wanted, ignorant or blind to the ecological consequences.

But while God's creation is certainly meant to provide for us, can we in conscience say that we have no responsibilities to it? As a result of human advances, species now become extinct with increasing frequency. Areas that once were home to many species are now desolate due to human rapacity.

Furthermore Americans need to be conscious of the fact that with less than one-third of the world's population we use more than two-thirds of the world's resources. Is this just, particularly when many of these resources come from underdeveloped countries at prices far below their true worth?

Also consider the question of the quality of life. Acid rain and air pollution already threaten to damage significantly our air and water. Hard questions demand action. Are we willing to proceed unheedful of the consequences or will we struggle with these issues, learning as a species to work in harmony with our environment? The answer's consequences will be experienced for generations to come. How grateful will our children be to us with a scorched, depleted, unhealthy world as their inheritance?

Humanity is a part of God's creation; we are inextricably joined with creation in a delicate web of interdependencies. That web is being threatened by our rampant industrialization and technology. A spirituality of stewardship is desperately needed today to lead us back to a saner and healthier relationship to our mother earth and her other creatures given into our care by God.

4J. How might one discern between different kinds of Christianity?

There are various shades of Christianity in our society today. How might a person go about discerning whether a particular Christian community is healthy and true to the Gospel?

Is what you hear from a Christian group really good news?
Often humans pervert the good news of the Gospel into bad
news. For the Gospel is indeed too good to be true. So we add
our own human element and flesh it out a little. But the first
meaning of Gospel is definitely good news. If it doesn't sound
like very good news, chances are that it isn't very Christian.

More talk of punishment and vengeance than of love and
forgiveness doesn't come from Jesus but from his followers.
The picture of God that we receive from some Christian groups
is quite angry and mean. We accept behavior from God that we
would not tolerate from another human being. But is this angry
God the loving Father that Jesus shows us? Is it even the God of
Israel? Jews, with only the notion of God in the Hebrew
Scriptures, have never pictured the holy tyrant that many
Christians proclaim.

St. Paul provides wonderful criteria for discerning the true
spirit. "By their fruits you shall know them," said Jesus.[26] We
can apply this to any group. In spite of saying some wonderful
things, how does the group act? The harvest of the Spirit is
love, joy, peace, patience, kindness, goodness, fidelity,
gentleness, and self-control.[27] Of course all communities and
people fail to live up to the Gospel in its fullness. But do they
acknowledge their failure and rejoice in God's forgiveness? Or
do they pretend perfection?

The Nicene Creed is a watershed of orthodoxy. It was
hammered out in the third century and accepted by the entire
Church of that time. Since then most Christians cherish it as the
definitive statement of Christian belief. Does this Christian
community hold to the Nicene Creed? Or does it deny certain
parts of the Creed?

---

26. Mt 7:16.
27. Gal 5:22–24.

The Creed is bigger than any one of the Christian Churches. It is held in common by Roman Catholics, Orthodox, Lutherans, Episcopalians, Methodists, Presbyterians and many others. A group that does not hold to the Creed sets itself against what is overwhelmingly held to be the most concise statement of Christian belief.

The Nicene Creed is a part of Christian history. What is the history of the group you are exploring? Every group has a history. Suspect those who deny it. The Catholic and other Churches are easy targets of criticism because their history is public and known. We have to answer for the Inquisition and the Crusades. And we should. The Church is made up of sinners.

If a group denies that it has a history, what is it hiding? Furthermore, do not accept what is told you without investigation. And what does it mean when one must trace one's history through heretical groups that have failed to weather the winds of time? Can this be the promise of Jesus to stand by his Church against even the gates of hell?[28]

What place does the group give to charity and compassion? Jesus was always compassionate, especially with the poor and outcast of his day. Charity has been a hallmark of Christianity throughout the ages. If the group seems more judgmental and haranguing than compassionate, or if its compassion appears limited to group members or is not an important part of the Gospel it practices, the group is listening to part of the Gospel rather than all of it.

Ask too how the money is spent. What portion goes toward charity to the poor? What portion is used to bolster the particular community? This is especially a matter for investigation if money forms a significant topic of preaching.

---

28. Mt 16:18–19.

Does belonging and practicing Christianity with this group provide real happiness? Happiness here is not an ecstatic high often associated with sudden conversion. There is nothing wrong with such a high so long as we realize that it is temporary and will give way to a calmer and more peaceful experience of happiness.

And does this happiness extend and flow out into the world or is it limited to the group? Does the group see itself as the last bastion of true Christianity? Such happiness is really a neurotic delusion. True Christian happiness flows out and touches all it meets in the charity and love with which God showers all creation.

Does this particular group invite or compel belief? Do they invite you to hear their message, and are they willing to dialogue about it? Or is it rather a hard-sell campaign with threats of hell if you do not accept things their way? Such a group is not the best representative of the good news. Jesus seldom threatened hellfire and damnation. Instead he healed, forgave and told stories of a loving God. A group that presents another kind of good news is not presenting Jesus' Gospel.

Does this group share the mind of Jesus? The Gospels are open for anyone to read and present a clear picture of Jesus. We see his ways of dealing with people. We learn his values. We come to understand the God he proclaims. Is this group of the same mind as Jesus? Or do they sound harsher, less forgiving, more demanding, more judgmental?

How does the group see itself in relation to the world? Christians are in the world but not of it. We are not against the world—we do not condemn it. We love the people in it and wish to help them find true happiness. We do not conform to the world in its ways and its thoughts. Our allegiance is to God's Kingdom and we attempt to live by its values.

As Christians we are a sign to the world of God's love. We are not a sign of its condemnation. And we are here to serve the world: not only to present it with the good news of Jesus Christ, but to love its people and serve them so that they may experience the goodness of God.

Other Questions

5A. Do Christians believe that the world will end?

This question was extremely important for the New Testament Church since it believed that the world would soon end with the second coming of Jesus. As time went by, it became necessary to rethink these beliefs, and some scholars believe that St. Luke's Gospel (including the Acts of the Apostles) was written to address this problem.

Of course the world did not end, nor did Christians go out of existence. They rethought their ideas. But belief in an end continues as part of the Christian legacy. Practically all Christians believe that the world will end, and that at that time Jesus will come again in glory to inaugurate the Kingdom of God.

While Catholics hold to the traditional doctrines of the end of the world and the return of Christ in glory, the Church itself holds no opinions when this will happen. And Catholic scholarship, rejecting literalism, does not read apocalyptic passages to deduce a game plan for the end time.

Rather the scholar attempts to understand how the original author meant his writing to be perceived by his audience.[1] And apocalyptic is a literary genre, arising with a group in crisis: in Israel it arose during Greek and Roman occupation, and for the early Christians it arose at the time of their persecutions.

---

1. See question 1D.

To this group the literature offers a simple theme of hope. It views history symbolically, interprets that history, and promises that, although the group is experiencing trouble today, the day of the Lord will make all well. The exotic imagery results from the extreme situation.

To see in these images a list of events on the way to Armageddon is to use the texts in a way never intended. Of course a catholic can choose to read the texts in this way. But to do so twists the original purpose and meaning.

An obsession with the end of the world influences how a person or group acts in the world. The Christian Church early abandoned its idea of imminent apocalypse in favor of seeing Jesus Christ as the center of history. The Church sometimes became too friendly with the world and its ways, but at her best she was in the world but not of it.

Christians realized that they had a mission in the world and to the world. We are to take the good news to all people. We are here as creation's stewards. Rejoicing in the beautiful world God has given us we enhance and preserve its beauty. Receiving a mandate of peace from Jesus we attempt to be peacemakers in the world. The world is not the be-all of our existence, but it is loved for what it is.

When people take a more other-worldly stance their other attitudes and actions are affected. Some, viewing apocalyptic as a prediction of events, take a fated view of things. If everything is predicted in the Bible, there is no sense trying to make peace: Armageddon is going to happen come what may. And since the Christian longs for the Kingdom, why not promote the way to Armageddon?

5B. Do Christians have to believe in hell?

Hell has been much with the Christian imagination at least since Dante and Bosch had their go at it. Fundamentalists would banish the great majority of the human race there for their inability to accept Jesus Christ as their personal Lord and Savior.

Catholics have always had a problem with this issue. It arises from two different images of God: on the one hand, God the justice-maker sending sinners to hell, on the other, God the shepherd going after the lost sheep. Does this God who goes solely by whether or not a person accepts Jesus sound like Jesus' God? It does not, and the Church has always suspected so. Confronted with all who do not believe in Jesus, rather than condemn them to hell, she found other ways in which they might be saved.[2] Indeed Dante in his hell is stricter than the official dogma ever was. (And in thinking of Dante we might consider that he had his own reasons for assigning people where he did, as do we all.)

But is there a hell? Catholicism is concerned about our free will. Is it possible for us to refuse God? If not, we do not really have free will. So hell is necessary if only for the possibility of refusing God and his Kingdom.

We have to believe in the existence of hell. We do not have to believe that anyone is there. And the Church has never declared that a person is in hell. She only declares that some people are in heaven in her naming of saints. The population of hell is anyone's guess—Dante's, Milton's or your own. Why not rather leave judgment to God as Jesus would have us do?[3]

What would hell be? It is the opposite of God and his Kingdom: the rejection of love so as to live in utter selfishness. Such a hell

---

2. See question 3F.
3. Mt 7:1.

is not limited to the afterlife. It is a possibility right here and now. These states do not start after death; we create them now. After death they are finally frozen for all eternity.

Of course we might also ask whether it is possible for a finite creature to reject infinitely an all-loving God. Might we not hope that in the end all creation will be won back to God's love?

5C. Isn't purgatory simply a Catholic invention?

While purgatory seems today one of the most rejected doctrines, among Catholics and non-Catholics, it is one of the best insights into the spiritual life. Purgatory is not found in Scripture, but arose out of the Church's meditation upon revelation.

Consider the problem. Taking the traditional reading of Scripture that one is either damned to an eternity of hell or rewarded with an eternity of heaven produces a quandary. Either most people are going to go to hell, or heaven is not going to be such a nifty place.

After all, if I and my friends with all our little faults and sins are going to get into heaven, what is so heavenly about it? Is there no real difference between the Christian who keeps his or her nose fairly clean and the saint transformed into an image of Christ? Keep the real estate values up and most of us are going to end up in hell. But that idea doesn't fit Jesus' image of God as our loving Father.[4] Open the doors of heaven to all us riffraff and what's heaven going to be like? More of the same we've come to know on earth.

For most of us a purgation of our sinful selves would be needed before we could become full members of God's Kingdom. That

---

4. See question 5B.

purifying should naturally come through the course of Christian life—through our gradual dying to ourselves so that Christ can live in us. But what about those (the majority) who merely slide through life, not taking the opportunity to grow significantly in holiness? Will we slip into the Kingdom with all our faults intact? Or will we undergo purification?

In her reflection the Church came to see this process of purgation as essential to passing over into the Kingdom of God, and since most of us have not completed the process by the time of our death the Church postulates that the process can be completed during and after death itself. This state came to be called purgatory.

The problem with all afterlife teachings is that we use our present experience and vocabulary to describe states of which as yet we have no experience. Thus it is easy to take the descriptions too literally, and that is just what has happened with hell, purgatory and heaven.

Each, instead of being a state of being as the Church defines them, solidifies into a place with a specific geography. Hell is in the center of the earth, heaven in the sky and purgatory wherever one can find room for it. Then outgrowing the literal images we find the whole concept faulty and reject it.

But are these terms faulty taken in their original sense of states of being? There are people on earth today who are living in hell. They are cut off from their fellows. They are turned in upon themselves and filled with selfishness. Are they happy?

Some have managed to move far into the Kingdom vision. Their lives are spent in love and service. Are they happy? Perhaps not, if regarded superficially. Mother Teresa and her followers in India live in poverty. But they radiate a happiness more profound than most of us have experienced. They are in heaven here on earth.

And what about the rest of us? We are not isolated in hells of our own creation. Yet we have not thrown our lot totally with God's Kingdom. We vacillate, torn between God and ego. At times we respond generously; at times we are stuck through fear in selfishness. Hopefully we use opportunities to move closer to the Kingdom, and as we do so we are purified of our selfishness. But we are not there yet. We are in purgatory. These ideas, far from simply being a description of the afterlife, shed light upon our present predicament.

There is real consolation in the doctrine of purgatory. It allows full scope to the mercy of God. What of the people who do not seem too concerned about the Kingdom? They are not necessarily evil or totally selfish. They are preoccupied. Purgatory allows them a place in the Kingdom.

Eastern spiritualities tackle the same question. Reincarnation can be seen as another response to it. If the person does not do the spiritual work in this life, then it must be done in subsequent incarnations. Christianity rejected the idea of reincarnation because it led to a feeling that this life is not crucially important. With the Christian insistence upon the value of this moment, the idea of purgatory provides the same consolation that the work will be accomplished without denigrating the importance of doing the work now. Isn't it better to experience the happiness of the Kingdom here and now in our life rather than waiting until this life is over?

5D. Does Scripture predict world events?

Hal Lindsey, a fundamentalist author, has written a number of books concerning biblical prediction of events preceding the end of the world. He applies certain biblical passages to contemporary situations to show that the world's end is imminent.

Scripture scholars today first try to determine what the original author of a piece of Scripture meant to say. What was the original situation? When was the work written? Whom does it address? What does the author intend? These are difficult questions and scholars often debate the fine points. But they agree that the Bible is not in the business of predicting events two thousand years in the future. To use it this way is to misuse it.

Most of the "predictive" passages come from a type of literature known as apocalyptic. This special literature arises during times of persecution. The most famous Old Testament example is the Book of Daniel. The author writes fairly late in Israel's history when she was subject to the Alexandrian empire. He places the time of the book at an earlier date during the Babylonian captivity—another crisis period. There the prophet Daniel (a fictional character) makes a number of predictions. Now most of the predictions have already occurred by the time of the book's writing—they are now history. The Babylonian empire has fallen to the Persians, who have been conquered by Alexander. The Antiochene occupation is the current situation. And Daniel predicts that this too shall fall, giving consolation to the people about that. And hope is basically what apocalyptic offers.

Taking this literature we can with imagination find all sorts of allusions to modern events and times. And throughout the centuries Christians have played this game. The major Christian apocalyptic is the Book of Revelation, in the form of a vision given to St. John. He sees visions in groups of seven—a holy number signifying completeness (seven days of the week). There is always a pause—a period of silence before the final image. There are six trumpets and then silence in heaven before the seventh.[5] The six signs refer to past events—the

---

5. Rv 8:6—9:21.

present Christian persecution corresponds to the period of silence—and the promise is that God will bring about his Kingdom soon with the seventh sign.

Of course there is much other imagery such as the vision of the beast and the number 666.[6] These have always fascinated Christians who throughout history have reckoned our enemies as the dreaded 666. Reformation Protestants showed that the Pope was 666, while at the same time Catholics argued that Luther or some other reformer was the beast. Hitler, Napoleon and anyone else who gathered enemies since has been played with so that his or her name adds up significantly.

So Hal Lindsey and his modern confreres are only part of a great and long (but hardly noble) tradition. And if the others were wrong, who is to say that Lindsey is right? Around the turn of the millennium the Christian world went through a tremendous end-of-the-world fever. Thousands were convinced that the final days were at hand and that signs like the bubonic plague were confirmation.

Our times in spite of atomic threat seem sane in comparison. And such thinking leads to a dangerous attitude. After all if the world is going to end no matter what we do because God has a preset doomsday clock, why should we worry about war or the bomb? It is inevitable one way or another. Such an attitude could lead us to give up our mission on behalf of peace. And we may be just the voice needed to keep the bombs from falling.

Christians are sent by God into the world. He does not hate the world or long for its destruction. It is his creation after all and he finds it good.[7] Rather than preparing for the end, Christians should seek ways of bringing peace, ways of granting all the world's peoples the rich life God has given. To read the

---

6. Rv 12:18—13:18.
7. Gn 1:3.

Scriptures in ways not intended is not only frivolous; it can be downright sinful.

5E. Are not the Marian doctrines (immaculate conception and the assumption) additions to the faith?

The immaculate conception and the assumption are not found in Scripture. They arose from reflection upon Mary and from traditions handed down in the early Church. The dogma of the assumption can be traced back to the third century. It states that after her death Mary was assumed body and soul into heaven. Thus she is already fully resurrected in heaven: a state we will share at the end of time.

The dogma of the immaculate conception developed in the Middle Ages from reflection upon Mary's role as the Savior's mother. Because of her role in bearing the Savior Mary was preserved free from sin from the moment of conception onward. She achieved this not on her own merits but through the redemption to be accomplished in Christ flowing backward in time.

These doctrines became an official part of Roman Catholic teaching at a time when Marian devotion had reached its peak. But they are not central teachings of the faith. And in today's Church devotion to Mary has assumed a more appropriate place in relation to Christ.

However it is important to see the significance of Mary for catholic Christianity. Much of the Christian world came to see Jesus primarily as the Son of God and as the coming judge who must act out of justice. Other aspects such as his mercy and compassion were overshadowed. Christianity became over-identified with the stern masculine qualities, ignoring the softer feminine elements. Some strains of Protestantism produced a harsh, cold picture of God.

In Catholicism, to counter this trend toward sternness, the image of Mary developed in popular piety. Here was a truly feminine figure filled with a mother's compassion. She ameliorated the experience of God and Jesus for a Church too enamored with justice and reason.

Yes, this was a development not grounded in Scripture. But nothing in Marian piety is against Scripture, and many elements arise from meditation on Old Testament texts such as the Rose of Sharon[8] and the figure of Wisdom.[9] And the Marian texts of the New Testament such as Luke's Magnificat[10] support the spirit of this development, since it in turn is based on the song of Hannah.[11]

The development of Marian piety preserved the fullness of the Gospel spirit—the reality of compassion and forgiveness, and the understanding of weakness—that our image of God had lost. As a result Catholicism was never reduced to the harsh judgmental God. Mary humanized the image of God.

With the reforms of the Second Vatican Council and a renewal of scriptural study and meditation within the Church, Catholics recognize these Marian qualities of compassion and mercy proper to Jesus himself. Once again Jesus became human and approachable. The figure of Mary recedes into the background.

Indeed the Council itself found a new role for Mary. By declaring her Mother of the Church it encouraged Catholics to see her in a new light. She is an image of the Church. Like the Church she gives birth, bringing Christ into the world. Like the Church she is preserved by Christ in holiness. And as with the

---

8. Song 2:1.
9. Prv 8:1–36.
10. Lk 1:46–55.
11. 1 Sam 2:1–10.

Church at the end of time, Mary was assumed body and soul into the Kingdom. In her we glimpse our own destination.

5F. Is the rosary a prayer of vain repetition?

This question, often leveled at Catholics, refers to an instruction of Jesus against prayer which through flowery words and images seeks to impress God.[12] He is against prayer as flattery. The rosary is not a prayer of flattery. And, understood correctly, it is a quite advanced form of meditation.

Catholicism allows a rich, full expression of prayer. Prayer is of course speaking to God. But there are other kinds of prayer as well. There is the prayer of silence and contemplation: a prayer of simply being in God's presence. Just as two people in love do not talk to one another all the time but pass to a point where they simply enjoy being in one another's presence, so the Christian may attain that state with God.

Meditative prayer also developed, and in Catholicism the rosary is a prominent example (the stations of the cross are another). In this prayer we enter into the stories of Jesus, savoring them and penetrating to a deeper understanding of their mysteries.

Jesus taught primarily through parables concerning the Kingdom of God. These point toward and afford us a glimpse of the Kingdom. After Easter the disciples recognized Jesus himself as the center of the Kingdom, and they began to add stories about Jesus to the stories he told.

A good story is inexhaustible. To hear it once doesn't mine its depths. We relish hearing favorite stories again no matter how many times we might have heard them, no matter how well we know them. In rehearing, a different light might be thrown on

---

12. Mt 6:7.

the story. We may recognize something which before eluded us. Or we may simply enjoy the experience once more.

Christians have always meditated upon the stories connected with Jesus. The rosary provides a format for this meditation. The mind is quieted by the use of the Hail Mary while we contemplate certain mysteries from the life of Jesus and Mary so that we may enter more fully into God's revelation and be transformed.

The repetitions are not to influence God or provide the one praying with power over God. Rather they quiet the mind and center our being upon God. People have attested to the peace which saying the rosary creates.

We see related kinds of prayer in other traditions. Indeed Islam, Hinduism and Buddhism have rosaries of their own. In Hinduism the mantra or holy word is similar to the Hail Mary and other words of power in Christianity (such as the name "Jesus," "Amen" and "Alleluia").

Of course the rosary or any form of prayer can be misused. But that is not the fault of the prayer but of the pray-er. As intended to be prayed the rosary is a powerful way of bringing the Christian into contact with Christ through meditation upon the great events of our salvation.

5G. Can a Christian be a humanist?

A humanist working for human values is striving for what is best in human nature. Granted the humanist does not have the whole picture—what Christ brings as grace is missing. Therefore elements of humanist philosophy are deficient and not in the best interests of humanity. But humanism can prepare the ground for Christianity.

Thus a catholic and a humanist might differ upon their belief
or non-belief in God (and there are many humanists who
believe in God). And they might disagree in a number of areas
because Christian humanism is informed by the spiritual and
supernatural values of Jesus, but in their basic commitment to
the importance of the human being they are agreed.

The catholic would argue that the fullest humanism is a
Christian humanism because only there are things seen in
proper perspective. Putting God in the picture saves humanity
from some serious errors. But it is impossible for a catholic not
to be a humanist. For we believe that God has revealed himself
to us in Jesus to teach us how to become fully human, and in
doing so he lifts us up to himself.

5H. Can a Christian be a Marxist or Communist?

No one institution has been more vocal in criticizing
communism than the Catholic Church. But when John XXIII
threw open the windows to dialogue with the modern world,
that dialogue included Marxists as well. In opening this
dialogue the Church recognized first that there are varieties of
communists. There are the Soviet Communists who have
created totalitarian states in Russia and elsewhere. But then
there are Marxists whose viewpoints are different from the
Soviet line. And there are socialists who are quite different
from communists.

In any dialogue it is necessary first to overcome stereotypes and
begin to share just what each believes and values. The Marxist
value of the worker and the oppressed certainly strikes a chord
among Christians. In Marxism Christians hear echoed the
prophets of old, addressing society on behalf of the voiceless.

Of course unanimity is not yet at hand. For a Christian can
never accept Marxist atheism. And Marxists have not

abandoned their critique of religion. But as dialogue continues Marxists see that the religion Marx criticized has indeed been transformed and now shares many of his dreams. Nor can Christians accept the Marxist tenet that the worker and the individual should be subordinate to the state. As John Paul II states,[13] both Marxism and capitalism fail because they exalt either the state or capital over the individual person. And finally Christians can never advocate violence because it goes against the Gospel, although the sin for violence must be placed not only upon the violent but upon those who maintain oppressive structures.

The situation in Latin America is crucial to developing Catholic thought. In these countries the Church has traditionally been a pillar of society aligning itself with the government and aristocracy against the poor. But people and clergy are being converted and see the struggle for freedom there as a continuation of the Gospel in the world. Christians find themselves allied with socialists and Marxists. And although there may be disagreements, all join together in the struggle for peace and development.

The Latin American situation is only beginning to make itself heard in the North American Church. But these people's struggle for justice is intricately tied to us and to our country. The coming decade may see the Catholic Church taking an ever more critical role of American policy in Latin America as we support the Latin American people in their struggle for liberation.

Can a Christian be a Marxist or a Communist? Not in the sense of adopting all the beliefs of traditional Marxism or Communism. But Christians are certainly called to carry liberation to oppressed peoples and to ally themselves with liberation movements so that all may come to share in the liberty of the children of God.

---

13. *Laborem exercens.*

Catholics are discovering friends outside the Church who share many of our basic dreams and values. We join in solidarity to achieve our common goals. To join with others does not involve giving up our own values or watering down our faith. It means cooperating with the liberating power of God wherever we find it.

5I. Can a Christian believe in evolution?

Fundamentalism first came to national prominence in the Scopes trial in Tennessee where Scopes, a teacher, was accused of teaching evolution in school against the supposed precepts of the Bible. Fundamentalists have persisted in their campaign against evolution and still attempt to force creationism into school science classes.

Evolution is a scientific theory to account for how we got here as a species. It is not a fact. It is not conclusively proven. Like all scientific theories it is the best explanation so far that fits the evidence at hand—notably the fossil record. While not a fact, it is regarded today quite seriously by most scientists involved in the investigation of our past.

Arising in the nineteenth century out of the theories of Darwin (although there are other theorists of evolution Darwin gets most of the credit), it aroused a good deal of controversy before becoming one of the great ideas of the early twentieth century—inspiring art (such as Shaw's *Man and Superman*) as well as advancing scientific knowledge. Positing a slow evolution of the human species from the ape, it went against current beliefs springing from the Book of Genesis that man is God's direct creation. At first most Christians had difficulty accepting these new ideas. Like most important discoveries evolution forced the world to reconsider a number of things.

Fundamentalists were only the most vocal in opposing evolution. The theory was no more accepted among other

Christians; certainly Catholics in the 1920's were not open to it. But it and other modern ideas forced Christians to re-examine the Bible. Just what does the Bible teach? And is the Bible free from error as previous generations had thought?[14]

Liberal Protestant Churches made peace with evolution rather quickly. They had already come to sense the Bible's limitations as a result of the growth of modern biblical scholarship in the nineteenth century. The Catholic Church at first sided against evolution. But with study and reflection Catholic scholars gradually formed a new understanding of Scripture, given official approval by Pope Pius XII in 1943.

Catholics acknowledged that Scripture does not intend to teach about history or science. It communicates God's revelation. To do so God uses the language and thought structures of the original biblical author. Through that language God communicates the truth he wishes to reveal. Thus the history, the science, and the other human knowledge in the Bible is not free from error or necessarily true. What is true is the God revealed in the Scriptures and his message to us.

Of course questions need to be addressed concerning the theory of evolution. For example, does the scriptural idea of the generation from one set of parents (Adam and Eve) conflict with a theory that postulates an emergence of human beings in different areas of the world? How would such a theory influence our understanding of original sin—as passed down by Adam and Eve to their descendants? Scholars wrestle with these questions, and it is generally accepted today that the overall theory of evolution is not necessarily against Christian revelation. Of course certain aspects of a specific theory may contain material contrary to Christian revelation.

A giant of modern Catholic thought developed a theology founded on the idea of evolution itself. Far from seeing

---

14. See question 1F.

evolution as evidence against Christianity Teilhard de Chardin saw evolution as a deeper understanding of what God was doing in Christ. Indeed Paul himself spoke of creation groaning in travail.[15] Teilhard's ideas were radical for their day and he was silenced by the Church. But since his death they have become accepted, and he is the inspiration behind many a modern theology of evolution in both Catholic and Protestant traditions.

5J. What might a Christian believe about other religions?

In the world where Christianity was born the only high religion was Judaism. And early Christianity had to come to grips with Israel and her rejection of Jesus as the Messiah. The best response is found in Paul's Letter to the Romans where he basically says that Israel's rejection of the Messiah does not alter her status with God, and is a mystery known only to God.[16] In other words there is no adequate answer to the question.

Unfortunately Christianity soon came up with another answer and contributed mightily to anti-semitism. The Jews rejecting Christ were accursed. In the modern world Christians have begun to be aware of their sin against the Jews and to recognize once more the tremendous debt Christianity owes Israel. Pope John XXIII spoke for the modern Church when he told the rabbi of Jerusalem: I am Joseph your brother. The Second Vatican Council in its Declaration on the non-Christian Religions made anti-semitism unacceptable for Catholics today.

The other religions at the time of the Church's founding were the various cults of the Roman Empire and the mystery cults imported from the East. None equaled the moral force or spiritual wisdom of Judaism and its offspring, Christianity. Partly for this reason Christianity swept the Roman Empire,

---

15. Rom 8:22.
16. Rom 11:25–32.

becoming the established religion within a mere three hundred years.

The next high religion Christianity faced was Islam in the Middle Ages. Islam has always had a fairly antagonistic relationship with Christianity, and the two religions warred— literally in the Crusades—with one another. In spite of this there was some influence between the two.

And Christianity for one was influenced by the Islamic renaissance. Through Islam Aristotle comes back to the West, forcing St. Thomas Aquinas to make him an acceptable basis for Christian theology. And there is some evidence that Francis of Assisi when he journeyed to the Middle East was influenced by Sufism—the mystical tradition of Islam. Certainly the reflowering of song, story and the rebirth of love mysticism in Christianity has antecedents in Sufism.

Not until the nineteenth century did Europeans or Americans come into direct contact with other high religions such as Buddhism or Hinduism in a way open to the wisdom of these traditions. Obviously a half-baked idea of a faith does not shed much light on the faith. It led to Romans believing that Christians were incestuous because they called one another brother and sister. And it led Europeans to have equally false ideas about Hinduism from the little they saw and then misunderstood in colonial India.

But the beginning of contact with other faiths in the late nineteenth and twentieth century created a quandary for some Christians. Of course many simply followed Paul's condemnation of the decadent paganism of his day and applied it to all other religion.

But other Christians began to study these traditions and found much beauty, truth and wisdom there. They were forced to consider how Christians should regard these other faiths. In the last few years many Christian bodies have begun not only to respect these great traditions but to dialogue and exchange with them. Although superficially what we say may seem to contradict one another, yet underlying the words and ideas are often profoundly similar experiences, values and viewpoints.

Catholicism has an easier time admitting the truth in other religions. For once Christianity moved from Israel to Rome, Christians were confronted with the great philosophies of Greece and Rome. How could these pagan philosophers have come so close to the truth?

Out of this questioning arose the idea of natural revelation. God is the Creator of the world. Thus everything in this world bears God's imprint. His creatures may come to know him through his creation, and ultimately through the crown of his creation: human reason. Thus Augustine saw seeds of Christ throughout the classical world. He read Plato and saw there a hinting at Christ similar to the prophets of the Old Testament. Christians even came to read Virgil's fourth Eclogue not as the paean to Augustus it was intended to be but as a hymn to Jesus Christ who came into the world at that time.

Through such reasoning the Church recognized the wisdom in classical learning and used it to ground the emerging Christian philosophy. In valuing this knowledge she also preserved it through the barbarous Dark Ages, making it available to us today. Indeed these early Christians took care to preserve even works they did not agree with such as Lucretius' poetry which argued against the idea of an afterlife. They demonstrate that Christians can be quite civilized about making room for alternative viewpoints.

Thus the Church that recognized seeds of Christ in the Greek philosophers can with the same reasoning grant a revelation of God in the other religions. And the Catholic Church did just that in the Second Vatican Council.[17] God can choose to reveal

---

17. Church in the Modern World.

himself whenever and wherever he chooses. We believe that he has done this in his fullness only in Jesus Christ. But this revelation does not restrict him. Certainly our vision of God received in Jesus does not show some stingy deity, but rather an extremely prodigal God willing to go to any extreme—even death on a cross—to reach us and establish a relationship with us.

We can see the footsteps of God in other faiths. And we can benefit from the insights and the practices of other religions as long as they do not deny our own faith. Indeed today catholics practice Zen meditation. There are Christian-Hindu monasteries in India. And Fr. Raimundo Panikkar has suggested that Indian philosophy might prove a better base for Christian theology than Aristotle.

Thomas Merton predicted that the twenty-first century would belong to two things: Christianity and Zen. Today these great traditions as well as others are meeting one another in a spirit of humble inquiry. Perhaps it is just this coming together of our world traditions that will provide the spiritual impetus needed to usher in a new age of the Spirit.